The CONSTITUTION of the UNITED STATES

An Unfolding Story

The
CONSTITUTION
of the UNITED STATES
An
Unfolding Story

second edition

Joseph T. Keenan
DePaul University

Brooks/ Cole Publishing Company

Pacific Grove, California

Acquisitions editor: *Leo Wiegman*
Production editor: *Gladys True*
Copyediting coordinator: *Jane Lightell*
Production manager: *Charles J. Hess*
Designers: *Michael Warrell, Diana Yost*
Compositor: *Weimer Typesetting Co., Inc.*
Typeface: *10/12 Times Roman*
Printer: *Arcata Graphics/Kingsport*

ISBN 0-534-10627-7
Former ISBN 0-256-06076-2

Library of Congress Catalog Card No. 87–51117

Printed in the United States of America

10 9 8 7 6 5 4 3

To Kitty and our nine "amendments"*

*Michael, Mary Anne, Patrick, Susan, Carol, Joe, Jr., Daniel, Kerry, and Christopher

Preface

It was Publisher David Follmer's idea. We met in his office in early June and agreed on a thorough revision of our highly successful 1975 edition of this little paperback. Next day, on the flight back to Arizona, I prepared chapter and subdivision sequences.

But perspiration and inspiration do not automatically follow preparation. My adjustment to retirement had been easy. Readjustment to old disciplines proved difficult. A month passed and I had not punched out a single paragraph.

Then inspiration struck swiftly, and at night. It came as I watched television and was transported in fancy by a glittering array of notables, by graceful tall ships, by spectacular fireworks, and by the intensity of the glow that sent patriotic shivers of pride through Americans from Hoboken to Honolulu. It was July 3, 1986—the evening of Let Freedom Ring Day of Liberty Weekend. Maybe I was stirred into action the next morning by Kitty's expert needling, "How many chapters have you finished?" But I like to think I was seduced by The Lady in the Harbor.

At any rate, this manuscript, like Yankee Doodle Dandy's life, began on the Fourth of July. That was when I realized that the Declaration of Independence was a glorious one-shot document; that Miss Liberty is a symbolic beacon of hope and opportunity. But the Constitution of the United States is a living, viable, continuing blueprint for a governmental way of life. That's when it came to me that I was indeed privileged to tell this story. My purpose will be fulfilled if it contributes to a wider knowledge of a world-class document.

Like Miss Liberty, this edition has undergone a complete facelift and an extensive wardrobe change. The pages are reduced in size, but have almost doubled in number. The "white spaces" have disappeared. In the interest of internal clarity, the previous edition's programming format has been replaced with sample exams at the end of each chapter.

Other new features:

Chapter 1, "The Road to Philadelphia," which sketches historical stepping stones from Hammurabi to the Articles of Confederation, has been considerably expanded.

"Those Bewildering Legal Citations" should no longer be bewildering—or downright intimidating. See Chapter 6.

Just as a supermarket is divided into Areas, then subdivided into divisions and Shelves, our Constitution is split up into Articles, Sections, and Paragraphs. The formula for finding things becomes, well, almost magical in Chapter 7.

From the standpoint of a history teacher, the delegates made one stupid mistake. See if you agree after reading "Did the Founding Fathers Goof?" in Chapter 7.

Study Tips for remembering the twenty-six amendments have been tested in my classroom. They work! Give me four minutes of your time two or three times a day for a week and you'll be amazed. What's more, the system of *association* works with phone numbers, grocery lists, birthdays, anything.

Chapter 5, on the Amendments, has been greatly expanded to include the many subtle ways the Constitution can be bypassed or "amended" unofficially.

We're proudest of the new chapter containing 16 "Famous Supreme Court Cases," conveniently briefed, which has been added at the suggestion of teachers. *Gideon* (Henry Fonda played him, remember?), *Miranda, Marbury, Roe, Baker*—most of the ones you want will be included. They've been tested on my 19-year-old Christopher and his friends, and should excite most other high school and beginning college students.

Most of the features which proved popular in 1975 are back, too. The Declaration of Independence, complete with an introductory essay, and the *full* text of the Articles of Confederation, accompanied by a running commentary. They're right where teachers said they wanted them—in the Appendix, not under separate cover in the library. Many teachers have also taken the time to say "Thank you" for the discussion of the Equal Rights Amendment.

Above all, the U.S. Constitution has a fascinating "biography," not unlike that of the neighborhood brat who marries the girl across the street and becomes the town's leading benefactor. Regardless of how well this edition succeeds in the classroom, the author will consider it a failure if it does not prove seductive to Lifetime Browser and Curious Soul—those inveterate snoopers of library and bookstore shelves who are simply looking for a good story.

Besides Curious Soul, this book is intended for: College students and high schoolers desiring a top grade on their Constitution exam; every alien contemplating U.S. citizenship; discussion groups—the Famous Cases, Q's & A's, and the ERA discussion are custom-made for provoking dialogue; and, students of History and Political Science; Education majors (they all have to take a Constitution exam), Business Law students, and law school freshmen looking for summer background reading—there'll be little time for it once classes begin.

So many were so helpful. DePaul's Dr. Gerald Kreyche led my cheering section. Two other DePaul professors, Judge Thomas Wynn and Sholem Singer, consistently used the book in class and constantly sent encouragement. Graydon Burton offered me the use of a computer at McKay Learning Center, Ricks College, Idaho, and was infinitely patient in his instructions. Congressman Bob Stump (Rep., AZ) provided information from Library of Congress sources. Jeanne Crawford of Arizona State University in Sun City was a great help. Distinguished Fulbright Scholar and Notre Dame Professor of Law Douglas Kmiec cheerfully volunteered his expertise. Rumors that he was coerced by my daughter, under threat of divorce, are unfounded.

From our first discussion, I knew folks at The Dorsey Press were solidly behind this effort, especially David Follmer, Leo Wiegman, Gail Kus, and Gladys True.

And we always try to save something special for dessert. Like a thanks to Bill Crawford. When he came into the DePaul University Bookstore in the mid-1970s as a salesman and vice-president, I asked him if he had a good paperback on the Constitution.

"No," he said. "So why don't you write one for us?"

Joseph T. Keenan
Sun City, AZ

Contents

The
CONSTITUTION
of the UNITED
STATES
An
Unfolding Story

1

The Road to Philadelphia

ANCIENT TIES

Once upon a time, a benevolent Ruler handed Moses two tablets containing ten common-sense rules for a better life.

Then there was Hammurabi. Centuries before Moses and some seventeen hundred years before Christ, his Code of Laws was posted prominently. Every Amorite understood the rules and consequences.

Fifteen hundred years after Hammurabi, Athenians of the Golden Age of Pericles set a brief but brilliant example of the kind of culture it was possible to create under a democracy, albeit one that excluded slaves, foreigners, and women. The Athenian Council of 500 (elected by lot and sometimes changed monthly) and the General Assembly, both under the control of a strong leader, were distant forerunners of the parliamentary system of government. But Greece was swiftly engulfed by Philip of Macedon. Philip's son, Alexander the Great, extended the empire into three continents. When Alexander died at age thirty-three, Rome swallowed his empire in three bites over three centuries—one bite per continent.

At the heyday of the *Pax Romana* (Peace of Rome), the Romans perfected the science of lawgiving and public administration, creating a legend for governing on a grand scale that is still remembered. Like its Athenian predecessors, the Roman Senate, especially in the prime of Cicero, offered another antiquarian example of a deliberative legislative body.

That's about it! If you're a historical detective, seeking even the flimsiest of precedents for the written American Constitution of 1787, you'll find little else

1

in the first four thousand years of recorded history. Blind, unforgiving absolutism dominated the ancient world.

FEUDAL TIES

When Roman government degenerated, then collapsed in 476 A.D., the Western world had a perfect example of what can happen under anarchy. For a thousand years the lords of the manor ruled their own self-sufficient bailiwicks, exacting labor from their lieges in return for protection, a rude hut, and a harsh, crib-to-coffin existence.

Still, the *grand jury of one's peers* stems from the English feudal period. And the Magna Carta (Great Charter) of 1215, cornerstone of English political freedom, was primarily a written agreement between king and barons to honor the terms of their implied feudal contract. It came about, not out of love or respect, but because of widespread distrust of King John, whose name is etched in history only because he was too deceitful and unscrupulous to be trusted with an oral agreement.

The century that spawned Magna Carta also witnessed the birth of the lively and still thriving Swiss democracy. The Swiss Confederacy today has evolved into 26 cantons to which citizens have formed strong parochial loyalties. At the federal level, voters elect an Assembly every four years; then, in referendums held every few months, citizens vote "aye" or "nay" on the Assembly's measures. As a pure form of participatory government, this 700-year-old experiment is unrivalled in the world family of nations, even though it was only 50% participatory. Women's suffrage was not instituted until 1972.

WESTPHALIA AND THE BIRTH OF THE NATION-STATE

If precedents for our modern form of government were virtually nonexistent in ancient and medieval history, they appear in abundance on the pages of English, continental and American history of the seventeenth century.

The modern nation-state developed from the Treaty of Westphalia, signed in 1648, at the end of the Thirty Years' War. The war was the last and most bitter and most destructive of Europe's religious wars.

At the time, much of Europe was a political mishmash of states, duchies, margravates, and principalities under the nominal direction of a prince of the Hapsburg family. Known as the Holy Roman Empire, it was neither holy nor Roman nor an empire. Its people had little in common except a harsh existence. It might better have been called "the Germanies."

The Thirty Years' War was a curious affair. Dynastic dreams triumphed over religious convictions. For some time a Protestant prince of Brandenburg aided the Catholics; the Catholic Cardinal Richelieu, regent for Louis XIII, funneled French support to the Protestants in the early stages. About 85 percent of all villages in the empire were devastated; two-thirds of all movable property just up and moved; vast acreages were laid waste; culture, the arts, manners, and education took a holiday. Even the winners were losers at the peace table at Westphalia.

A nation-state of the modern type could never have thrived within the sprawling confines of the administrative monster known as the Holy Roman Empire. But with the empire's destruction, a few states from within began to emerge individually with the stuff that turns patches of land and people into *nations*—a common ethnicity, a common or dominant religion, a common language, common problems and aspirations, and, of course, a common sovereign free from outside obligations. From the ashes of Westphalia, Catholic Austria under the Hapsburgs and Protestant Prussia under the Hohenzollerns slowly emerged. Within a century they would become powers to be reckoned with.

SEVENTEENTH CENTURY STEPPING STONES

The seventeenth century, which opened Europe to the principle of the nation-state, also witnessed a brisk demand for the type of guaranteed rights and participatory government that were to be incorporated into the American Constitution of 1787. The demand was reflected in the decapitation of an English king and a limitation of powers of the crown; it was expressed by English subjects in the newly established American colonies; it was inflamed by the writings of political and social philosophers; it infiltrated the organizational structure of the Calvinist church; its spirit sailed with the *Mayflower*.

Government by Compact

If the historical precedent for a written constitution is not to be found fully in the English governmental system, the principle of a written "compact" or agreement among people on how they were to be governed is clearly ingrained in Calvinist church organizational theory. (In America the Dutch and German Reform Churches and all Presbyterian branches were offshoots of Calvinism.)

In his *Institutes of the Christian Religion*, blueprint of Calvinist doctrine, John Calvin acknowledged that the church cannot even come into being except by common consent.

Many little "compact" forms of government emerged in the American colonies. By far the best known had its origin in the cabin of the *Mayflower*. Shortly before landing on Plymouth Rock in November 1620, the men of the ship "solemnly and mutually in the presence of God and of one another," wrote out the Mayflower Compact by which they agreed to "covenant and combine ourselves together into a civil body politic."

This principle of government by written agreement was accepted sixteen years later by Roger Williams and his tiny group of rebels who left Massachusetts for Providence, Rhode Island. Several other Rhode Island towns followed suit.

Fundamental Orders of Connecticut

In 1639 the colonists of Windsor, Wethersfield, and Hartford, Connecticut, consented to be ruled under a written constitution. The document specified that the freemen would gather annually to choose a governor and a board of magistrates. Each town would have four representatives at a general court that would also be attended by the governor and magistrates. The general court clearly dominated the governor.

The document became known as the Fundamental Orders of Connecticut and is *generally considered to be the first modern written constitution*.

The Instrument of Government

England's only noteworthy attempt at government under a written constitution began fourteen years later, in 1653, when Puritan leaders formed a Protectorate under a document known as the *Instrument of Government. Among the nations of the world the Instrument of Government was the first written constitution of the modern type. It may be recognized as a reasonable prototype of the American Constitution of 1787*.

The executive power was wielded by a Lord Protector, Oliver Cromwell, subject to the advice of a Council of State. Legislative authority was vested in a Parliament apportioned somewhat imperfectly according to population. The Lord Protector's legislative veto could be overridden by a simple majority of the 460-member Parliament, thirty of whom were from Ireland and thirty from Scotland. Catholics and Royalists in the recent civil war were disenfranchised, and religious freedom was granted to all except Catholics and Episcopalians.

Established by military men, the Instrument almost immediately degenerated into a harsh military rule. It could not have been more unpopular in papist-hating England if it had called for His Holiness to cross the channel and rule by proclamation from the pulpit of Canterbury. Within three years the document was scuttled and succeeded by a new constitution, the *Humble Petition and Advice*, equally inefficient, unpopular, and inconsequential.

One common denominator lurks behind the Mayflower Compact, the compact executed by Roger Williams in Rhode Island, the Fundamental Orders of Connecticut, and the Instrument of Government: *all were illegal*. The *Mayflower* Pilgrims realized they were landing on forbidden ground, for their grant was in Virginia; Roger Williams, banished from Massachusetts Bay, did not receive a legal charter for Providence until 1644, eight years after his compact was signed; the Connecticut River planters had neither title nor patent to their territory; and the men who set up the Instrument of Government were constitutional imposters. History may never know for sure whether all four of these constitutional experiments were merely conscious efforts to justify illegal actions.

The English to this day have no written constitution. Their structure of government and cherished rights are rooted in custom, tradition, the common law, Acts of Parliament, judicial interpretations, and in numerous documents, some of which were executed at point of sword as well as pen.

The Restoration

Oliver Cromwell died in 1658, and two years later Charles II, Parliament, and the Anglican church returned to power under the Restoration.

The new king was the handsome, lazy, yet capable Charles II. His father, Charles I, had been forced in 1628 to sign the historic Petition of Right, limiting the king's power, a document he promptly ignored. Charles I was beheaded in 1649 after being tried by Parliament. Charles II consorted with a string of mistresses and entrusted many decisions of government to a group of five poker-playing, womanizing, whiskey-drinking cronies. By agreeing to the Restoration Settlement he clearly implied that the crown would henceforth be subject to limitations of power. Without a gun being fired and without a drop of blood being shed, the Restoration was a people's victory as glorious as any battle on land or the high seas.

Incidentally, the first initial of the names of Charles II's little group—Clifford, Arlington, Buckingham, Ashley, and Lauderdale—spelled the anagram CABAL. This is the origin of the word used today to denote a tight, little, unofficial ruling group. The group met in a small room. A common English term for such a room is *cabinet*. Thus, a second word had its genesis.

The Glorious Revolution

The Glorious (and bloodless) Revolution of 1688 and the historic English Bill of Rights climaxed the long and bitter seventeenth century struggle for power between crown and Parliament. Fearing a Catholic succession, the Whigs accomplished their Glorious Revolution when they overthrew James II and brought William of Orange and Mary (James' Protestant daughter by a first marriage) to the English throne. As a result, the world-famous Bill of Rights was adopted the following year, guaranteeing the Protestant succession for all time, listing basic constitutional rights, and detailing the charges against James II. Several provisions in the English Bill of Rights are almost identical to the guarantees in the U.S. Bill of Rights.

The English struggle to limit the power of the Stuarts recalls such names and terms as The Gunpowder Plot; The Period of Personal Rule, when Charles

I struggled along for eleven years without calling Parliament; the Cromwellian Revolution; divine right of kings; John Bate and John Hampden, who risked jail by refusing to pay taxes not levied by Parliament; John Pym and Edward Hyde, who asserted Parliament's power against Charles I; and the courageous Sir Edward Coke, the brilliant jurist who dared to state that even kings were subject to the law.

Out of the long seventeenth century clash of wills and arms and ideals, Parliament emerged the unquestioned victor. The Glorious Revolution of 1688 proved that Parliament could make a king; no one doubted that it could also unmake a king.

The struggle occurred during the height of the American colonization period, and the colonists learned remarkably well. The causes that prompted the Whigs to rebel against James Stuart in 1688 were much the same as those that motivated the American colonists to revolt against George III a century later, prompting a British observer to remark during the Revolutionary War, "By God, they are whipping us with our own belt straps."

Chief political and philosophical apologist for the English action in dethroning James II was John Locke (1632–1704), whose first and second *Treatises of Government* (1690) were written to justify the Glorious Revolution. Locke's words spread far beyond England, however, and found receptive ears among the Founding Fathers. His theories of a "compact system of government," of a "social contract," and of the "right to rebellion," detailed in *The Second Treatise of Government*, were copied by Thomas Jefferson in the Declaration of Independence.

Men enter the world totally free, according to Locke. They are unfettered by any chains of authority and are endowed by their Creator with such "natural" rights as life, liberty, and property. But because of the imperfections of man, the state of total serenity and security in nature is not attainable without a few "ground rules." Thus, men voluntarily surrender a part of their freedom in order to protect their lives and possessions. By agreement (or compact) they choose a way of government headed by one of their own. When this compact is broken, the people have not only the right, but the *duty*, to rebel.

In the art of revolution and in the struggle for basic liberties, the English proved brilliant teachers. These "lessons learned" deserve to be listed in any mosaic of precedents leading to the Constitutional Convention of 1787.

THE EIGHTEENTH CENTURY—ENLIGHTENMENT AND REBELLION

An undercurrent of rebellion coursed through the last half of the eighteenth century, marching to the accompaniment of various Enlightenment intellectuals, including the French philosophes. Elaborating on the themes expressed earlier by John Locke, the philosophes glorified nature, natural science, and natural law; questioned the source of sovereignty; and sang the praises of the individual. Their ranks included Rousseau, Voltaire, Montesquieu, D'Alambert, and Diderot. Their instruments were the acid pen and the barbed phrase.

It was a century when a few Americans developed pangs of conscience. In 1761 Quakers were forbidden to have anything to do with slavery; in 1774 Dr. Benjamin Rush formed an abolition society. A slaveholder by the name of Thomas Jefferson doubted the right of any man to enslave another.

It was a period when a group of economic theorists known as Physiocrats revered land as the source of all nourishment and wealth; when Adam Smith railed against monopolies, trade restrictions and artificial burdens; and when Europe's Seven Years' War spread out over three continents and the high seas. It was a time when Thomas Paine roused the American patriots with his widely read pamphlets, which called for independence from England and the establishment of a strong federal union. The eighteenth century spawned a Boston Tea Party, a *Declaration of Independence*, a French *Declaration of the Rights of Man and of the Citizen*, and accelerated use of the guillotine.

In a period of five years, from 1776 through 1780, the eighteenth century witnessed the establishment of eleven written U.S. state constitutions. In 1781, the thirteen states combined to form a government under a document called the Articles of Confederation. Then, in 1786, there occurred two events known in history as Shays' Rebellion and the Annapolis Convention. These were the events that led directly to the demise of the Articles of Confederation and to the Constitutional Convention of 1787.

Problems with the administration of the Articles of Confederation arose both during and after the Revolutionary War. But it was not until the new nation experienced an economic recession about 1785 that public unrest surfaced. In most states the ferment was merely reflected in belt-tightening and indignant letters to the editor. In New Hampshire, however, the governor was forced to call out the militia to disperse a mob gathered at the state capitol in an effort to force the state to issue more paper money. The New Hampshire incident was easily squelched, but the ineptitude of the Articles was dramatized by a more serious incident in Massachusetts.

Shays' Rebellion

Thirty-nine year old Daniel Shays, who fought at Bunker Hill and rose to the rank of captain in the Revolutionary War, was reasonably typical of hundreds of returning veterans who lived on farms in western Massachusetts. Disillusioned because he had to wait for his back pay, caught between the hard-money squeeze and the state's demand for extortionate land taxes payable in specie (coin), Shays looked to the state for relief. But there was no one to whom he could even protest. Many of the districts of western Massachusetts were without effective representation in the assembly in Boston because the districts were either too poor to send representatives or because the men who would best represent them could not meet the legislative property qualifications. The merchant and seafaring members of the Boston assembly ignored the pleas of the western farmers and adjourned in July 1786.

Shut out at the state house, the western farmers called unofficial county conventions to talk things over and fan the fires of discontent. Quickly, their disenchantment was translated into action. They attacked and closed several civil courts where foreclosure proceedings were taking away scores of farms. When ringleaders were arrested and charged with inciting riots, the furious farmers proceeded to shut down the criminal courts.

This was too much for Governor Bowdoin. In January 1787, he called the militia to put down the rebel cause, which by this time was headed by Shays. Sporadically, the fighting continued for more than a month before Shays' pathetic "army" of perhaps 1,200 men was routed.

The Annapolis Convention

When a dispute arose over navigation rights on the Potomac River, representatives of Virginia and Maryland met for a discussion at George Washington's home at Mount Vernon in 1785. Their problem, they readily agreed, had to do with the inability of the Confederation Congress to handle interstate commerce.

As a result, Virginia invited all thirteen states to meet in Annapolis in September 1786. Nine accepted, but only New York, New Jersey, Pennsylvania, Delaware, and Virginia actually sent delegates. Without a quorum, the proceedings could be merely advisory. When the five states agreed that the Articles needed revising, Alexander Hamilton of New York moved that all the states meet in Philadelphia the following spring and take action "to render the Constitution . . . adequate to the exigencies of the Union." The motion was carried.

John Dickenson of Delaware served as chairman at Annapolis. James Madison took copious notes. Seven states had already chosen delegates when, on February 21, 1787, the Confederation Congress—spurred by concern over Shays' Rebellion—passed an almost identical resolution. The Annapolis Convention, in effect, was a warm-up for the most famous constitutional convention in American (or world) history.

State Constitutions

The U.S. Constitution that was to emerge in 1787 followed a series of charters forged by individual states during the preceding decade. In the first five years of the American Revolution, eleven states graphically crowned their declared breakaway from George III by writing constitutions. Only Rhode Island and Connecticut, satisfied with their existing charters, did not adopt new constitutions.

Brevity was a common characteristic of these documents. Generally, only the skeletal bones were provided, and the legislatures were empowered to pack in the flesh.

Another universal feature reflected the colonists' fear of the governor. Even though he no longer would be a representative of the king or the proprietor, the governor was in most cases accorded a very short term of office, and his powers were pointedly reduced in relation to those of the legislature.

These state constitution makers were extremely conscious of the basic freedoms they were fighting for at the time. As a result, seven of the eleven constitutions contained bills of rights.

Features such as checks and balances, reduced powers of the chief executive, and concern for cherished liberties were carefully inscribed in all the state constitutions. As night follows day, it was certain that any new *national* constitution would carry the same guarantees.

Before looking into the proceedings of the Constitutional Convention of 1787, let us take a look at the Articles of Confederation to understand better why James Madison and a few others were insistent on a clean break from the past.

ARTICLES OF CONFEDERATION—OR OF FAITH?

From 1781 to 1789 our country operated under a written constitution called the Articles of Confederation. Adopted during the Revolutionary War, the Articles established a unicameral legislature, with each state having one vote, regardless of population. The Articles guaranteed the states' sovereignty and reserved for them all powers not granted specifically to Congress. Congress had among its powers the authority to declare war, make treaties, issue money, handle Indian affairs, and establish post offices.

The Articles were inadequate for several reasons. There was no chief executive, no federal judiciary, no power of taxation, no provision for regulation of commerce, no power to enforce. Congress could request troops from the states, but had no authority to raise or equip an army or navy of its own. Making polite "requisitions" to the states for funds and manpower, and billing itself a "firm league of friendship," the fledgling Congress should have called its guiding charter the Articles of Faith, not Confederation.

Despite these faults, the Articles might have succeeded but for one fatal weakness: the requirement of *unanimous approval for any amendment*. This doomed all movements for change, for it was virtually impossible to get thirteen states to agree on anything. The Founding Fathers discovered this even before the Articles officially went into effect, for the principle of unanimous consent was also required for ratification. For lack of a single vote—Maryland's—ratification was held up for two critical war years.

These shortcomings were not oversights. The governmental ship of state teetered precariously to the states-rights side for only one reason: that's what

Table 1   The Articles of Confederation and the Constitution   (How the Constitution corrected weaknesses in the Articles)

Articles	Constitution
States are sovereign, retaining all power not accorded to federal government.	Article VI establishes the Constitution and the laws and treaties of the U.S. as the supreme laws of the land. Article I grants Congress both enumerated and implied powers.
No executive.	Article II provides for a president to execute the laws and serve as commander in chief.
No federal judiciary.	Article III establishes the Supreme Court and gives Congress the power to create other federal courts as necessary.
One-house legislature, with members chosen by state legislatures, and each state having one vote, regardless of population.	Article I establishes House of Representatives and Senate. Number of representatives per state varies according to population; each state has equal number of senators. Representatives chosen by the people, and senators chosen by state legislatures. (Since amended to provide for direct election of senators.)
Congress has no power to tax, but must requisition funds from the states.	Article I, Section 8 establishes Congress' power to tax.
Congress has no power to raise an army or navy of the United states.	Article I, Section 8 gives Congress the power to raise and support an army and navy.
Congress has no power to regulate foreign or interstate commerce.	Article I, Section 8 gives Congress authority to regulate foreign and interstate commerce.
Amendments to Articles require unanimous approval of all states.	Amendments to the Constitution require approval of three-fourths of the states.

the people wanted. State sovereignty was a cherished prerogative, one for which the colonists were fighting and dying at the time the Articles were adopted, one of the ideals that had inspired their forefathers to attempt the hazardous journey to the new land. Implanted in the mind of every American was a congenital distrust of the strong executive (king), his central court system, his calloused tax collectors, and his military collaborators.

As the proud new nation began to engage in diplomatic negotiations, however, it was kept humble by the burdensome restrictions of the Articles. Lacking armed might and international respect, American ships suffered piracy and insult on the high seas. At home, with no *national* tariff policy, manufacturers were in danger of being wiped out by cheap imports. Congress had little power to settle disputes among the states, and even less control over the vast frontier. Spaniard, Englishman, and Indian menaced frontiers defended only by local vigilante groups or pussycat state militias. Thirteen sets of state laws occasionally created frustrating, bewildering, and often comical legal situations.

Among those who blushed in embarrassment was John Adams, minister to England, who is said to have broached the subject of a commercial treaty to a member of the English Foreign Office.

"Would you like one treaty or thirteen, Mr. Adams?" asked the British diplomat.

Another who turned crimson was George Washington. As commander in chief of the Continental Army, he had been subject to the whims of thirteen masters, spread up and down the Atlantic coast.

And we have already seen how constitutional weaknesses brought on Shays' Rebellion and the Annapolis Convention.

Yet the Articles of Confederation deserves much praise. As the first viable written national constitution, it served as a landmark, blazing the way for the modern republican form of government. Thomas Jefferson hailed the new government as the best government that ever existed, and a model of what a loose confederation should be. Despite stultifying birth defects, the Articles of Confederation stoutly carried the fledgling United States through the Revolutionary War. And by clearly outlining powers to be held by a central government, it acted as an important precursor to the Constitution of 1787. Perhaps most important was the fact that, as John Marshall observed, the Articles preserved the idea of a federal union until national wisdom could adopt a more efficient system.

Now that we understand the background of the parent, it is time to sit in on the pregnancy and birth of the present Constitution of the United States.

QUESTIONS

1. Was the Athenian example of democracy a true democracy?
2. Who were the finest public administrators of the ancient world?
3. What was Magna Carta all about?
4. How did the Thirty Years' War pave the way for the modern nation-state?
5. Why is the English Instrument of Government, a dismal failure, remembered in history?
6. What constitutional-type action did the men of the *Mayflower* make?
7. What development evolved from the Thirty Years' War and Treaty of Westphalia?
8. When was the English constitution written?
9. Give a theological example of compact government.
10. Name an early Connecticut forerunner of our constitution.
11. How are the Instrument of Government, the Mayflower Compact, and the Rhode Island Compact alike?

12. Why does constitutional history pay attention to the Fundamental Orders?

13. What did the English Restoration restore?

14. What was the significance of the Glorious Revolution and English Bill of Rights?

15. Why was the Annapolis Convention important?

16. What was the single most glaring fault of the Articles?

17. What type of legislature did the Articles have?

18. What type of people were Daniel Shays and his followers?

19. Why were the Articles so aggressively states'-rights oriented?

20. Why was Shays' Rebellion dangerous?

21. What two common words had their origin in the unofficial rule of Charles II and his fun-loving cronies?

22. What lessons did seventeenth century Englishmen teach Americans?

See Answers to Questions, pp. 169–70.

2

The Philadelphia Story

WHAT MANNER OF MEN?

Seventy-four delegates were named to the Constitutional Convention by twelve state legislatures. (Rhode Island did not participate.) Of the seventy-four, only fifty-five presented credentials in Philadelphia. What manner of men were the fifty-five who spent the summer of 1787 in steamy Independence Hall?

James MacGregor Burns, a gifted phrasemaker, calls them "the well-bred, the well-fed, the well-read, and the well-wed." Well said! In a day when grammar school education was an achievement, twenty-nine of the thirty-nine who signed the final document were university educated. They were professors, governors, legislators, financiers, doctors, lawyers, planters, merchants. Most had legislative experience with the Continental Congress or the Congress under the Articles of Confederation. Of the thirty-nine signers, George Washington and James Madison would move on to the presidency; John Rutledge, James Wilson, John Blair, John Dickinson, and William Paterson would become Supreme Court justices; Alexander Hamilton and James McHenry would become cabinet members. Others would serve as congressmen, governors, and judges.

Despite Benjamin Franklin's eighty-one years, it was a remarkably young group, representing a young nation of young people—a pattern out of step with the popular concept of a group of doddering, white-haired Founding Fathers. The nation itself, if its birthday can be determined as July 4, 1776, was only eleven years old; more than half of its four million citizens were under sixteen years of age, and the average age of the delegates was about forty-three. Of the thirty-nine signers, fifteen were in their twenties or early thirties.

13

Since each state was to have one vote, there was no rule as to the number of delegates each state could send. Pennsylvania, perhaps because the expense was minimal for a delegate living at home, sent the most—eight. Virginia also named eight, but Patrick Henry remained at home and was not replaced.

By a stroke of fortune, Virginia had been the first to choose delegates, setting a magnificent example. We shall never know how many states looked at the names—George Washington, James Madison, George Mason, John Blair, George Wythe, and Governor Edmund Randolph—and resolved, if we may borrow a greeting card slogan, to send their very best. Nor will we ever know how many prominent statesmen agreed to come just for the honor of sitting in such distinguished company.

"Dear God, do not send little men," a speaker warned the Connecticut legislature. The state responded by sending only giants. "A Solomon, a Daniel, and a Saul," as one chauvinist put it: Oliver Ellsworth, chief justice of the state's supreme court; William Samuel Johnson, a former justice and recipient of a Doctorate of Laws from Oxford; and Roger Sherman, who would become a prominent architect of the Connecticut Compromise.

No greater patriot nor abler civil servant answered the call than Alexander Hamilton of New York's three-man delegation. Yet frustration burdened this West Indian-born delegate to such an extent that he sometimes stayed in bed. His colleagues were Robert Yates and John Lansing, a pair of practical politicians. Jealous guardians of the principle of state sovereignty, they outvoted Hamilton, two to one, on every vital issue. When Lansing and Yates left on July 5, never to return, Hamilton was still unable to cast a vote for New York. The state no longer had a quorum.

Maryland named a first-rate delegation headed by Charles Carroll. But the men elected to stay home and fight a move to print a large issue of paper money. A substitute slate, headed by Luther Martin, arrived several weeks late. It was not equal to the original.

Massachusetts' Rufus King, widely known for his eloquence, William Paterson of New Jersey, John Rutledge and C. C. Pinckney of South Carolina, and John Dickinson of Delaware added integrity and experience to this gathering of minds.

Pennsylvania was most cooperative. Her eight-man delegation included Franklin, who disregarded an aggravated case of gout to be carried into the convention on a sedan chair; James Wilson, a scholar, debater, and an outstanding constitutionalist; and the polished Morris brothers, Robert and Gouverneur.

But no list of fifty-five people selected by twelve sets of politicians can be perfect. A number of delegates were simply good men with flexible minds who did a workmanlike job for their country. A few were politicians first and statesmen only when it was convenient. A few others simply didn't belong on the pages of the Philadelphia Story. Some critics have charged that certain delegates were motivated by greed, because they held devalued securities of the existing government, and the establishment of a strong government would increase the value of their holdings. It seems apparent, however, that most of the delegates had less selfish motives for their participation in the convention

Several thousand miles of ocean kept three distinguished statesmen away. Thomas Paine, whose *Common Sense* and *The Crisis* made him known as "the voice of the American Revolution," was in England. Thomas Jefferson was serving as minister to France, and John Adams was similarly occupied in London. Patrick Henry was elected a delegate, but declined to serve. Madison correctly guessed that Henry wished to be free to oppose; a year later the famous orator bitterly denounced the document signed at Philadelphia. Because of his strong Federalist principles, the highly qualified John Jay was passed up by Anti-Federalist New York. Samuel Adams and John Hancock were not named as delegates.

A nest of male WASPS!* That's how the 1787 assemblage at Independence Hall may appear through the enlightened lens of a 1987 telescope. There were no blacks, no Jews, no Indians, no women, no members of the working class, and only two Catholics. But history must be read through the perspective of the times in which it was made. In agrarian, postrevolutionary America, labor was scattered and unorganized. The large migrations from Catholic European countries had not yet taken place, so that the two Catholic delegates may even have been overrepresentative. Jews were an even tinier minority. Even if there had *not* been racial and gender discrimination, the number of blacks, Indians, and women who were qualified through education and first-hand legal and legislative experience was minimal. And if the Convention was WASPish, well, America was WASPish.

In Rhode Island, which was fearful of having to pay its considerable debts with a sound *national* currency, the agrarian majority was printing paper money by the ream in Providence and refused to send a delegation. "Rogue Island," as one of its many detractors called it, was also the last state to ratify, holding off until May 1790, thirty-two months after the convention adjourned and sixteen months after the Constitution became the law of the land.

Historian Charles Beard published his controversial *An Economic Interpretation of the Constitution* in 1913. His thesis was that the affluence of the convention delegates resulted in a pro-property bias in the Constitution.

In the late 1950s and early 1960s, Beard's findings were subjected to scholarly scrutiny. Forrest MacDonald's *We the People*, for instance, questioned the methodology, claiming Beard asked the wrong questions and got some wrong answers. MacDonald argued that shipping, manufacturing, professional, merchant, and planter factions, far from acting in concert, canceled out each other's vote as often as they offered support.

Slaves, like horses, were property in 1787. In this respect, the Constitution was strongly pro-property. Many delegates, including George Washington, were

---

*White, Anglo-Saxon, Protestants.

slaveholders. The Constitution did not grant citizenship to slaves, and counted them as only a fraction of a person for purposes of representation. Although some delegates opposed slavery and wanted to outlaw it under the new government, they failed to press the issue. There is no element of a slave code in the document; there is not even the word *slave* or *slavery*. Using circumlocutions, the framers of the Constitution evaded the whole issue of slavery. Most historical realists believe that insistence upon an antislavery stand might have precluded *any* constitution.

Despite the fact that delegates were appointed by politicians (state legislators) and despite absence of a few standouts such as Jefferson and Adams, it was a remarkable group that gathered in Philadelphia at the State House, now called Independence Hall.

For the most part, they were young, they were dedicated, they were talented, and there can be no quarreling with the results they achieved: they drafted the most durable and the most successful constitution in the history of the world.

No other written constitution is even close to celebrating a bicentennial.

SETTING THE SCENE

James Madison was the first visiting delegate to arrive, coming on May 3, eleven days ahead of time. There was something prophetic about his early appearance, for in everything he did, constitution-wise, the diminutive "Jemmy" was at least eleven days ahead of everyone else. A hint of his capability could have been found in his resume: graduate of the College of New Jersey (later renamed Princeton), member of the Virginia legislature and of the Virginia State Constitutional Convention, delegate to the Annapolis Convention, member of the Confederation Congress, omniverous reader, scholar, author, friend of Jefferson. It seemed that for half his thirty-six years he had been preparing for that memorable summer of '87.

Few others were serious about answering the opening call to order. Some have suggested that long legislative experience accustomed the delegates to expect delays and early haggling over inconsequentials. Heavy rains, poor road conditions, and light purses were common excuses. A carriage ride from the more distant states averaged two to three weeks.

One who did make it on time was George Washington, who later would be chosen convention president. The fifty-five-year-old former commander in chief, escorted by a troop of light horse, arrived on Sunday, May 13, and immediately paid a courtesy call on Benjamin Franklin. The sight of these two legendary figures excited a gathering crowd and created a climate of optimism. It was as if the two popular heroes had galloped up Market Street on white chargers, waving white hats and shouting, "We can do it!"

By the next morning, only the local Pennsylvanians and a quorum of Virginians were on hand, necessitating a delay until May 25. But the delay was not a total loss. The Virginians met almost every morning, then joined Pennsylvania delegates in the afternoon for further informal discussions. It was during this period that the critical Virginia Resolves, variously known as the Randolph Plan, the Virginia Plan, or the Large-States Plan, were formulated. The chief organizer of these discussions? Mr. Madison, of course. It was an earlier letter from Madison to Washington that was the genesis of the plan.

We wonder if any of our readers can imagine the explosion today if a *national* political convention of any importance rejected the press credentials of CBS, *the New York Times*, and *Time* magazine, then failed to seat a single delegate with the endorsement of the NAACP, NOW, or the UAW.

This, in essence, was what happened at the Constitutional Convention that established the world's noblest democracy. Troopers guarded the State House doors. No press credentials were honored. A strict secrecy oath was imposed. It prevailed for almost four months.

Official records were not disclosed for sixty years. Even so, the notes of James Madison, published fifty years later, have been of much greater historical value than the bloodless *Journal* of minutes, motions, amendments, and procedural pronouncements. William Pierce of Georgia made delightful little personal commentaries on his fellow delegates, which have afforded valuable insights to historians. Dr. William Johnson's diary is also helpful. At least half a dozen others published their observations. But none approached the scholarly, orderly presentation of Madison, who transcribed his notes in the evening, while they were still fresh. He did not miss a single session, and fellow delegates furthered his project by handing him copies of their speeches. History is deeply in his debt.

Parliamentary politeness prevailed. The gentlemen addressed each other and the chair with old world courtesy and formality. In an entire summer of impassioned debate, there were no oaths, obscenities, vindictive personal attacks, or threats of filibuster. By agreement, once a delegate had addressed the convention he could not again speak on that subject until all the delegates had been given a chance to speak. The rules banned whispering, or even reading a newspaper while a fellow delegate was speaking. The clerk did not take the "ayes" and "nays" of individual members, thus allowing for simple changes of mind, without embarrassment, at a later time. Votes were cast by *state*, and when even-numbered state delegations split, the state's vote was not counted.

So that they might speak freely and informally, the delegates often turned the convention into a session of the committee of the whole. This was a centuries-old ploy of English Parliaments, whereby the speaker would step down from the chair, removing the gavel or mace, symbolic of the monarchical presence and authority, and turn the meeting over to a surrogate (substitute) member. With the gavel removed, no official record would be taken and the king would not be informed. When George Washington stepped down in Philadelphia, Nathaniel Gorham of Massachusetts presided over the committee of the whole.

RESOLUTION OF THE
ARTICLES OF CONFEDERATION CONGRESS
Adopted February 21, 1787

Resolved, That in the opinion of Congress, it is expedient, that on the second Monday in May next, a Convention of Delegates, who shall have been appointed by the several States, be held at Philadelphia, for the sole and express purpose of revising the Articles of Confederation, and reporting to Congress and the several Legislatures, such alterations and provisions therein, as shall, when agreed to in Congress, and confirmed by the States, render the federal Constitution adequate to the exigencies of Government, and the preservation of the Union.

There were seventy-nine working days of seven hours each, plus a great deal of "homework" at night. The Confederation Congress made no provision for payment. Some states provided remuneration; others did not. Fortunately, most delegates were wealthy. When New Hampshire could not afford to send representatives, delegate John Langdon agreed to pick up the tab.

At no time were more than eleven states represented in a single meeting, and seldom were there more than thirty delegates present. The fruitful work was performed in committee by about twelve men who were directed, cajoled, pushed, and inspired always by the intense and gifted delegate from Virginia and true "father of the Constitution," James Madison.

To illustrate how a few men dominated, four men addressed the convention a total of 640 times—Gouverneur Morris, 173; James Wilson, 168; James Madison, 161; and Roger Sherman, 138. Except for his remarks as presiding officer, George Washington spoke only once.

Though the east chamber of the Pennsylvanis State House was pleasant and reasonably cool, the weather was often intensely hot and humid, with scarcely enough breeze to riffle the cigar smoke. Not the least of the decisions was whether to open the windows, for the portholes that admitted fresh air also let in swarms of flies and mosquitoes.

There were, of course, no air conditioners, refrigerators, or electric fans. Mail was frustratingly slow; research, letter-writing, and committee work made the days long. Excerpts from letters leaves the impression that mere participation in the convention and living in a Philadelphia boarding house in the summer of '87 should have put a delegate in line for a Purple Heart.

The fifty-five delegates came and went, absented by anger, poverty, frustration, disappointment, and hangover, or kept away by illness, personal affairs, and business interests. The New Hampshire delegation arrived July 23, delayed two months by the hole in the treasury. John Mercer of Maryland was the last delegate to present credentials, appearing on August 6 when much of the work was already accomplished.

GAVEL TO GAVEL

The convention opened Friday, May 25, twelve days late. Friday and Saturday were devoted to organizational chores. Washington was unanimously elected president of the convention; Georgia's William Jackson was chosen secretary; Virginia's able George "Chancellor" Wythe was named to head the important Rules Committee.

Delegates, upon being introduced, rose to present credentials. It is in the meticulous wording of the small-state credentials that we sense the first official undercurrent of apprehensiveness that almost scuttled the good ship Constitution on the Beach of Sovereignty. Terms such as *by the grace of Almighty God, free, independent, proud,* and *Sovereign* (one could almost sense the capitalization and italicizing of the *Sovereign*) abounded. Some credentials carefully limited their holders, stressing the words of the resolution of the Confederation Congress (above). Delaware delegates were forbidden to change the principle of one-state-one-vote-regardless-of-size.

The Virginia Plan

The "bomb" was dropped the following Monday (May 28) by Governor Edmund Randolph of Virginia. In an address that took more than three hours, the tall, handsome, aristocratic Virginian presented the fifteen Virginia Resolves, the nucleus of the blueprint that came to be known as the Virginia Plan. So tactfully and logically did the young statesman accomplish his task that few heard the detonation, and the waves of dissent were mere ripples.

The convention then resolved that the following day it would turn itself into a committee of the whole to debate the Virginia Plan as long as necessary, to the exclusion of all other business.

This was an historic decision. It meant that the Articles of Confederation guidelines were out the window, for the Virginia Plan proposed a major overhaul of the structure of the government. It meant that the pretense of amending the Articles was over—squelched in one brisk, unanimous motion. It meant that the Federalists had carried the day. It would come to mean the end of loose confederation rule.

From May 30 to June 19 the committee of the whole debated the merits of the Virginia Plan, threshing out each point line by line, many times word by word. The Virginia Plan provided for a strong central government and called for:

1. A legislature of *two houses*, members of whom would be elected on the basis of the number of free inhabitants or of wealth. The lower house would be elected by the people; the upper house would be elected by the lower house; members would not be eligible for reelection.

2. A chief executive, who might be either an individual or a committee, elected by members of the two houses; the executive would not be eligible for reelection.

3. A supreme court of limited jurisdiction. The executive and supreme court would share jointly a "revision" or veto power.

4. Amending power to be vested in the *people*, not in the two houses or in the executive.

5. The legislature would have power to annul state laws.

If the small-states delegates had not noticed the detonation of May 28, they distinctly heard the one on June 11 when the convention approved proportional representation for both houses. This was the supreme crusher—the very thing the Delaware delegates were forbidden to countenance, the heart of the undercurrent of suspicion between the big guys and the little guys.

The New Jersey Plan

It was this shock wave that galvanized the small states into action. By June 15, they were ready to counterattack. William Paterson of New Jersey requested permission to present the New Jersey Plan. This plan provided for the following:

1. A one-house Congress *with each state having one vote*. Members of Congress would be chosen by the state legislatures. In addition to its existing rights, Congress would have the power to tax, to regulate interstate commerce, to levy import duties, and to devise means to force states to comply with requisitions.

2. A plural executive, elected by Congress and subject to removal by Congress or a majority of the states.

3. A supreme court with limited jurisdiction, to be appointed by the executive.

4. Acts of Congress and federal treaties would be the law of the land, requiring state compliance.

Although the New Jersey Plan clearly expanded the role of the national government, in practice, it merely embroidered upon the Articles of Confederation. The power of the national government would continue to rest with the states.

The New Jersey Plan was defeated, seven to three, after spirited debate. Nevertheless, the small states delegates were far from surrender. United, they held the vote that would force an acceptable compromise.

For the record, two other plans were presented. On May 29 Charles Pinckney presented his own personal plan for union. It was never seriously considered. Although a supporter of a strong central government such as the one which was eventually adopted, his later claim that he had almost single-handedly drafted the American Constitution is generally discredited. Some reports say that the South Carolinian was too young, too brash. Others contend his "Pinckney Draught" was given short shrift because it was presented late in the day when the delegates were anxious to get out of the stuffy State House. No genuine copy of the original survives, and Pinckney himself could not remember all the details when questioned a few years later.

Alexander Hamilton also presented a plan, calling for an upper house and an executive elected for life. But a constitution patterned after the British House of Lords and King had no chance. Hamilton did not attract a single supporter.

The Connecticut Compromise

The tension brought about by defeat of the New Jersey Plan was intensified when the subject of representation for both houses on the basis of population was renewed. An inflamed Luther Martin harangued the delegates for two days on the necessity for state equality in any federated network. The small states contended that proportional representation in both houses would put them at the mercy of the large states. They feared the large states would combine and form a dominant faction, completely controlling the new Congress.

On the other hand, Madison argued that future political alignments would probably be drawn along geographic or economic lines, with large and small states joining to form factions according to sectional interests.

The impasse seemed insurmountable. A barbed phrase, a slur, a misunderstood wisecrack—that's all that was needed to send enough small-states delegates packing to prevent a quorum. The fate of the nation hung in the balance.

This was the moment when Benjamin Franklin described the assembly as ". . . groping as it were in the dark to find political truth, and scarce able to distinguish it when presented to us . . ." Asking, ". . . how has it happened, Sir, that we have not hitherto once thought of humbly applying to the Father of lights to illuminate our understanding?" he moved that each session be opened with a prayer.

The venerable patriot then offered this memorable insight into his personal philosophy:

> I have lived, Sir, a long time, and the longer I live, the more convincing
> proofs I see of this truth—that God governs in the affairs of men. And if

a sparrow cannot fall to the ground without His notice, is it probable that an empire can rise without His aid?

Finally, a suggestion was adopted that a committee composed of one member from each state be appointed to work out a compromise. Staunch states' righters such as Luther Martin, Robert Yates, and William Paterson were among those named by their states to slug it out in committee.

Out of the committee report of July 5, the Great Compromise was hatched. Though often called the Connecticut Compromise, because of the work of Oliver Ellsworth and Roger Sherman, the term is a misnomer. Several others contributed. It provided for:

1. Equal representation in the upper house
2. Proportional membership in the lower house on the basis of one member per forty thousand inhabitants. Population, not property, was to be the sole basis of representation.

Acceptance of the Connecticut Compromise was the turning point of the convention. Many problems remained, but reasonable men now could find reasonable ways of surmounting them. Throughout the give and take of those sultry summer days, a single theme hummed through the minds of the small-state and states' rights delegates: "We have not sold our people down the stream; no matter what happens we will have two votes in the upper house."

The Connecticut Compromise paved the way for the "essential" three-fifths compromise on slavery as worked out in Article 1, Section 2, Paragraph 3. It proved to be an act of expediency which would lead, 74 years later, to a civil war.

The Final Draft

When all points were resolved, the twenty-three Articles were given to a committee of style, composed of William Samuel Johnson, chairman, Rufus King, Alexander Hamilton, James Madison, and Gouverneur Morris. The committee labored from September 8 to 12, reducing the twenty-three Articles to seven, simplifying, clarifying, changing the order, but retaining the original intent.

All members of the committee had a hand in the preparation of the details of the completed draft, but it was the thirty-five-year-old Gouverneur Morris who is credited with providing the clear, graceful, legalistic prose that still distinguishes this remarkable document. Tall, aristocratic, member of a wealthy and socially prominent New York family, openly contemptuous of democracy, Morris labored over the phraseology with the mind of a skilled lawyer, the heart of a philosopher, and the soul of a poet.

The completed draft was presented to the convention on September 12, and immediately drew scores of objections—Elbridge Gerry alone expressed eleven. After much debate but little alteration the Constitution of the United States was accepted and signed on September 17 by thirty-nine of the forty-two members present. Only Gerry, Mason, and Randolph declined to affix signatures. With a covering letter by George Washington, it was sent to the Articles of Confederation Congress, where it was received with considerable shock.

But the real job was just beginning.

RECOMMENDED READING ON THE CONVENTION AND RATIFICATION:

Bowen, Catherine Drinker. *Miracle at Philadelphia*. New York: Little Brown, 1987. A Book-of-the-Month Club selection.

Farrand, Max. *Framing of the Constitution of the U.S.* New Haven, Conn.: Yale University Press, 1962.

Van Doren, Carl, *The Great Rehearsal*. New York: Penguin, 1986.

Burns, James MacGregor. *Heritage of Liberty*, New York: Alfred A. Knopf, 1982. One chapter.

QUESTIONS

1. What was the average age of the Founding Fathers?
2. Who was the oldest delegate?
3. Why was it fortunate that Virginia was first to select delegates?
4. Who presented the Virginia Plan?
5. Why was Alexander Hamilton frustrated?
6. Who served as president of the convention?
7. Who wrote *An Economic Interpretation of the Constitution*?
8. What was his thesis?
9. Name a few famous Americans who did not participate at Philadelphia.
10. Were the proceedings democratic?
11. What is a committee of the whole?
12. Who presented the Small-States, or New Jersey, Plan?
13. What single action probably saved the Constitution?
14. What was Hamilton's plan patterned after?
15. Which delegate was chiefly responsible for the clear, legalistic prose of the Constitution?
16. What was Patrick Henry's role?
17. Who is known as "The Father of the Constitution?"
18. Why did the New Hampshire delegation arrive a month late?
19. How did the Constitution, prior to the Thirteenth, Fourteenth, and Fifteenth amendments, treat slaves?
20. What crucial decision was made in the first week of the convention?

See Answers to Questions, pp. 170–71.

3

Ratification

THE KEY WORD—SOVEREIGNTY

> sov-er-eign-ty 1. Supremacy of authority or rule, as exercised by a sovereign or a sovereign state. 2. Royal rank, authority, or power. 3. Complete independence and self-government. 4. A territory existing as an independent state.*

If we were permitted to add another definition, it would read:

> 5. Something the states had to give up—in part—in order to establish the Constitution of the United States.

The key word at Philadelphia had always been *sovereignty*. Surrender of it haunted the minds of militant states' righters; proper distribution of it challenged the wits of all who favored a powerful central government.

When the convention adjourned many delegates had the unenviable chore of going home and explaining why they had voted to trade away certain cherished prerogatives.

It was concern for *sovereignty* that caused the colonists to dump the tea in Boston Harbor, that prompted Jefferson to blister George III in the Declaration of Independence, and triggered "the shot heard 'round the world," setting off the Revolutionary War.

The American Heritage Dictionary of the English Language (New York: American Heritage Publishing, 1969).

24

It was this obsession with *sovereignty* that almost scuttled the noble plan for a new Constitution of the United States.

It would be concern for *sovereignty*, with all its subtle meanings, that would highlight the struggle for ratification.

Make no mistake about it, the struggle would be a bitter one!

THE MECHANICS OF RATIFICATION

The Confederation Congress looked upon the new Constitution with all the enthusiasm a firmly entrenched board of directors might look upon a surprise proposal to reorganize the corporation. Nevertheless (but without a kind word or a "God bless you") the Congress, reinforced by the return of ten of its members who had been delegates at Philadelphia, promptly voted to submit the proposal to the several states.

The state legislatures, in turn, could vote to call ratification conventions composed of delegates chosen by the people. Delegates were not always bound by the votes of their constituents and occasionally changed their minds after listening to the debates or the persuasive efforts of fellow delegates.

There is no question but that ratification by "We, the people" was a noble concept, establishing the fountainhead of sovereignty out of deep faith in the will of the great democratic majority. But many contend that it was less of a noble concept than a practical political necessity.

"Suppose the Constitution was submitted to the Confederation Congress or to the state legislatures," theorized one skeptic. "Do you think those gentlemen would have voted themselves out of a job?"

Article VII, the ratification article, required ratification by nine states. With Rhode Island's position predetermined (true to form, she did not call a convention until long after the question was settled), this meant nine out of twelve, not nine out of thirteen.

WHO COULD VOTE—THE ELITE MINORITY

The vote for ratification of the noblest of all democratic constitutions was every bit as undemocratic as the proceedings of the convention that had drafted that Constitution.

It must be remembered that these were *state* referendums. The emancipated suffrage proposed in the new Constitution had no bearing in these elections. State regulations applied. In eleven states, property qualifications would disenfranchise from one-fourth to two-thirds of all adult males. Residency and religious restrictions would further cut into these figures. In Virginia, South Carolina, and Georgia, blacks were excluded. The religious requirements, known as Test Acts, sometimes disenfranchised Roman Catholics; in Georgia, atheists were denied the suffrage.

Since women were never considered as potential voters, the various restrictions sometimes excluded five-sixths of all adults. Still, apathy and ignorance, particularly in the hinterlands, were the most effective censors, keeping from 60 to 80 percent of the privileged eligible minority from the polls. Of Pennsylvania's 430,000 citizens, 70,000 were eligible and only 13,000 voted; of Maryland's 320,000 residents, 25,000 were privileged to cast ballots, but only 6,000 bothered to do so. More than half of these were from the populated districts, primarily Baltimore, where the maritime interests looked forward to pleasant sailing under a single flag that would promote free-flowing trade.

All this in the most important election in the history of the United States!

Only one state, New York, granted general manhood suffrage for the constitutional referendum. And this for a good reason. The patrician class of New York overwhelmingly opposed the Constitution. They believed they could control the ballots of enough servants, sharecroppers, tenants, and employees to swing defeat. Indeed, if ballots had been counted individually, the Constitution could never have made it in New York. But the Poughkeepsie Convention was something less than a textbook example of representative democracy at work. The area we now call metropolitan New York, with fewer than ninety thousand citizens, was represented by twenty-three delegates; the "upstate" area, representing more than a quarter million people, had only forty.

THE OPPOSING SIDES

In the battle over ratification, those who favored the Constitution became known as Federalists. Those opposed were called Anti-Federalists, a negative term that many resented. In fact, many of the so-called Anti-Federalists recognized the need for a stronger national government. They simply objected to what this specific Constitution said—or did not say.

A leading Anti-Federalist argument pointed to the absence of a bill of rights in the proposed Constitution. The fear of losing precious personal liberties was a powerful weapon in the Anti-Federalists' arsenal. The issue developed into a bargaining chip in more than one state convention, as we shall see.

The Anti-Federalists also expressed concern about the proposed structure of the new government. Some feared that power would be concentrated in the hands of a few, and the Senate, in particular, would evolve into an aristocracy of the wealthy and the well-known. They questioned how a powerful national government could deal effectively with the diverse interests of a population spread across a vast—and expanding—territory. They foresaw that a Congress with the power to make all "necessary and proper" laws eventually would reduce the states to powerless satellites.

The campaign for approval by the states raged over a ten month period, roughly from October 1787, when the first legislatures met to set dates and issue calls for conventions, to the following August, by which time eleven states had ratified. *Raged* seems the proper verb, for emotions ran high and the participants played for keeps. A new way of life hung in the balance. Cherished prerogatives would have to be surrendered. Many believed that the dearly purchased freedoms of the Revolutionary War would be endangered.

Quickly, the Founding Fathers perceived that it was one thing to put a new Constitution down on a piece of paper and something else to sell that document to a nation of skeptical buyers.

When the Philadelphia Story finally trickled through to the average man on the street (or farm), he likened it to an instance where a group of carpenters had been called upon to add a dormer, a walk-in closet, and a pantry, and then, without permission of the absentee owner, decided to tear down the farmhouse and build a new one from scratch. How else could he reconcile a totally new structure of government with instructions to make suggestions on how to update the Articles? Even if he tended to approve the fresh approach, he was skeptical of the cloak of secrecy under which it was hatched.

Clearly, the American public needed convincing.

In addition to the general philosophical arguments put forth by the Federalists and Anti-Federalists, an array of arguments, pro and con, developed around more narrow concerns. All the forces and special interests that had interacted at the Philadelphia convention made themselves known in the campaign, plus many more: creditors who wanted payment in hard money and debtors who wished to pay off in devalued paper; manufacturers, planters, merchants, slaveholders, and seagoing interests; men who feared the Indians; men who wished to grab cheap western land; men who did not want the West colonized; people who exacted a living collecting river tolls and people who wanted to sail goods toll free; lawyers who stood to lose lucrative state contracts; congressmen who could be ratified right out of a job; rural people who feared the intolerance of metropolitan ballots; and citizens who feared that the ten-square-mile district to be set aside as the permanent home of the federal government would become a walled fortress from which squadrons of federal soldiers would march out to enforce federal regulations and the payment of federal taxes.

James Wilson summarized the opposition in this manner: "Every person who either enjoys or expects to enjoy a piece of profit under the present establishment will object to the proposed innovation."

Generally, the coastal areas would vote "aye" and the interior "nay"; small states, unable to exist independently and pleased with the compromise that gave them equal representation in the Senate, would approve more readily and with greater majorities than their big-state brothers; city dwellers, merchants, plantation owners, real estate speculators, people of affluence, and people who dealt in interstate commerce were inclined to favor. So were those who feared the British in Canada, the French in Louisiana, the Spanish in Florida, and the Indians in Georgia.

Laborers, small farmers, villagers, and the people of the frontier were usually opposed. Farmers, believing their fortunes (and mortgages) were tied to the adulterated dollar, opposed the sound money features that constitutionalism was certain to bring. Many "squatters" feared they might have to pay for lands that they had merely preempted. And they looked upon the professional land grabbers, who might be encouraged by the Constitution, as they might look upon foxes in their hen houses.

There were enough exceptions to these patterns, however, to make such generalizations dangerous. New York, North Carolina, and Rhode Island were coastal states with strong Anti-Federalist sentiments. Some interior communities dependent upon the free flow of river traffic were militantly Federalist. Backwoods Georgia, for reasons we shall see, favored ratification just as eagerly as the tidewater (coastal) region.

THE FEDERALISTS' ROAD TO VICTORY

The Federalists eventually won over a skeptical nation for a variety of reasons. One of the most important was that the Constitution offered a concrete program to deal with the multitude of problems the young nation faced. The Anti-Federalists had no alternative at the ready. The Federalists could paint a convincing picture of disunity, economic chaos—even reconquest by Britain— if the nation did not pull together quickly under a strong federal charter.

The cards of ratification were stacked in favor of the Federalists in other ways as well. America was a rural nation. Bad roads and the sheer nuisance of hitching up Old Dobbin would keep thousands of Anti-Federalist farmers away from the polls, while poor communications and the necessity of working long hours in the fields discouraged any organized Anti-Federalist campaigning in agricultural communities.

Even the weatherman dealt from the bottom of the deck. Wherever bad weather prevailed on election day, the rural vote was affected to a greater extent than that of the city.

The formula for selecting delegates also served the Federalist cause. Delegates to the state constitutional conventions were selected on the same proportional basis as were members of state assemblies. With few exceptions, rural and backwater areas were grossly underrepresented in the state assemblies, and this underrepresentation would carry over in the state ratification conventions.

There's no question that the influence of distinguished men greatly helped the Federalists. The average eligible voter was undoubtedly confused by the complex issues of ratification. In such a position, he must have found great comfort in the roll call of men who announced for ratification. It was a glittering list.

How could the old commander in chief, George Washington, ever do anything to scuttle the country for which he fought so valiantly? From Paris, Thomas Jefferson gave enthusiastic approval. How could anyone go wrong agreeing with the author of *The Declaration of Independence* and the nation's top intellectual? This new way of government can't be too bad, can it, if wise old Ben Franklin says we need it? You have to go along with people like Adams, Hamilton, Ellsworth, Wilson, Madison.

These are some of the thoughts and questions that must have entered voters' minds. History has no convenient, hard and fast quantitative records, but the conclusions reached by a majority of "undecideds" seem quite obvious.

Even the refusal of Governor Edmund Randolph to sign the Constitution did not help the opposition, for Randolph publicly repudiated the Anti-Federalists. One version had it that the handsome young Virginian hadn't signed the Constitution because he knew he had a promising career and feared repercussions later if the new government was not successful. Or he may have been disappointed in the compromises made in his Virginia Plan. It is also a matter of record that he was disturbed by the Constitution's stand on slavery. If the latter is the case, he was indeed a remarkably foresighted young man.

THE FEDERALIST PAPERS

From the hundreds of speeches, sermons, debates, pamphlets, editorials, books, and letters to the editor, one enduring piece of literature emerged—*The Federalist Papers*. A series of eighty-five essays aimed at persuading New York voters to favor the Constitution began appearing in the New York press on October 27, 1787, and continued periodically until May. They were widely reprinted. Under the *nom de plume* of "Publius," the essays were the work of John Jay, who wrote five, Madison, who probably wrote twenty-nine, and Hamilton, usually credited with authorship of fifty-one.

As clear, reasoned statements of the anatomy and metabolism of representative government, *The Federalist Papers* have no peer in world literature. Judges, congressmen, presidents, and diplomats have used them as guidelines for almost two hundred years. American political scientists refer to them as they would the *Bible*. They have been translated into many languages, studied worldwide, and have been influential in the formation of many modern constitutional forms of government.

Yet it is one of the ironies of history that *The Federalist Papers* probably had little direct influence in their time. Then, as now, few voters were swayed by low-key reasoning. Slogans, epithets, and ballyhoo probably persuaded more voters than these truly classic political analyses. The immediate effect of *The Federalist Papers* was indirectly profound because they convinced the respected intellectual leaders, who in turn rallied the voters.

RATIFICATION ROLL CALL

Three states registered quick, unanimous votes in favor of ratification: Delaware, New Jersey, and Georgia. The larger states had more to lose and more people to vent their feelings than the smaller states. Thus, the most bitter and

Here are a few excerpts from some of James Madison's writings in *The Federalist Papers*. In the first he argues persuasively for a large union as the best means for controlling factions. In the second and third, he addresses the common error of "confounding of a republic with a democracy."

The regulation of these various and interfering interests forms the principal task of modern legislation.

. . . the same advantage which a republic has over a democracy, in controlling the effects of faction, is enjoyed by a large over a small republic—is enjoyed by the Union over the States composing it.

. . . The influence of factious leaders may kindle a flame within their particular States, but will be unable to spread to a general conflagration through the other States.

Federalist #10

It is, that in a democracy the people exercise the government in person; in a republic they administer it by their representatives. . . . Under the confusion of names, it has been an easy task to transfer to a republic observations applicable to a democracy only.

Federalist #14

. . . we may define a republic to be . . . a government which . . . is administered by persons holding their offices during pleasure, for a limited period, or during good behavior.

Federalist #39

most newsworthy campaigns for ratification took place in Virginia, Pennsylvania, Massachusetts, and New York.

Let's take a closer look, in chronological order, at what went on at the various state conventions.

Delaware

The promise of equal representation for all states in the Senate was enough to convince Delaware of the wisdom of supporting the Constitution. The state won the distinction of being the first to ratify, with a unanimous vote on December 7, 1787.

Pennsylvania

Pennsylvania was first to hear of the Constitution, first to call a ratification convention, and was beaten by Delaware by only a few days for the honor of being first to ratify.

Thomas Mifflin, a delegate to the Constitutional Convention, gave the Pennsylvania legislature a sneak preview of the new document. On September 18, the day after the Constitutional Convention adjourned, he read the proposed document to the unicameral Pennsylvania legislature. Reactions were instantaneous and violent on both sides.

George Clymer, a member of the Pennsylvania legislature who had been a delegate, made the motion to call a state convention within twenty-four hours after the Confederation Congress sent the Constitution to the states. The votes for passage clearly existed. But with adjournment set for the following day, and with an election around the corner, Anti-Federalists in the assembly plotted the politics of procrastination. The November election, they hoped, might return an Assembly opposed to ratification.

A recess was achieved and when the afternoon session was called to order enough Anti-Federalists were absent to thwart a quorum call. The sergeant at arms, sent to fetch the absentees, reported he was unable to "haul them out of their hole."

On Saturday, the 29th, following a night of drinking and demonstrating, a band of overzealous citizens battered the windows of "Mr. Boyd's house," an Anti-Federalist hangout, and literally hauled two struggling assemblymen to the state house, where their sullen, silent presence was properly recorded by the clerk. With a quorum thus obtained, a convention call was issued by a vote of 45 to 2.

The campaign that followed was noisy and violent, as small townsmen, farmers, and backwoodsmen voiced their uncertainties. The doddering Franklin assured the doubters that their fears were groundless, but it was the eloquent and statesmanlike James Wilson who proved to be Pennsylvania's strongest and most effective champion of constitutionalism. He dwelt on the many checks and balances designed to thwart any grab for power by a single man or conspirational group of small states. He noted that the Senate, where the small states might gang up on the large ones, would be unable to railroad legislation without consent of the House, where Pennsylvania would wield the power of several small states. The president would have veto power over the Congress and the Congress in turn held a sort of reverse veto power over the president.

Despite the considerable stir created by opponents, the Constitution carried handily, 46 to 23, in the roll call of December 12, making Pennsylvania the second state to ratify.

New Jersey

Like Delaware, New Jersey was won over by the Connecticut Compromise, with its guarantee of equal representation in the Senate for large and small states alike. New Jersey's convention convened on December 11, and the delegates chalked up a unanimous vote in favor of ratification a week later, on

December 18. New Jersey thus became the third state to fall in line behind the Constitution.

Georgia

One clause in the preamble: (to) "provide for the common defense" was the bait that hooked Georgia. Savannah was a fortified city and the countryside shivered in fear of the Creek Indians. Others might debate theory and sovereignty and liberties infringed upon. Georgians needed the new Constitution and friendly federal troops—on the double.

George Washington clearly foresaw the issue: "If a weak State with the Indians on its back and the Spanish on its flank does not see the necessity of a General Government there must I think be wickedness or insanity in the way."

There was nothing in the Georgians' way. They voted unanimously in favor of ratification on January 2, 1788.

Connecticut

Connecticut was fifth to approve (on January 9), and no one summarized the advantages to the state better than Oliver Ellsworth. Pointing out Connecticut's geographical position, he noted that New York collected possibly £80,000 in import duties annually and that Connecticut paid approximately one-third of this amount. He also recalled how Connecticut promptly paid her wartime requisition taxes under the Articles of Confederation while other states reneged and got away with it under an impotent central authority. The vote was 128 to 40.

Massachusetts

There could be no union without populous Massachusetts, where a bitter constitutional tea party was waged for four weeks.

The province of Maine, which hoped to break away from Massachusetts and become an independent state, was solidly opposed. So were the delegates from the Berkshire area, where Captain Daniel Shays and his men had so recently raised so much turbulence (twenty-nine of the delegates had fought with Shays); so were the paper money people, the small farmers, and most of the tiny inland towns.

The coastal towns were Federalist. And the Federalists, with such stalwarts as Rufus King, Nathaniel Gorham, and former governor Bowdoin, were better organized.

Of the 355 delegates, 60 percent or more probably came to Boston on January 9 opposed. If the Federalists were to have any chance at all, they would need the hearty support of Samuel Adams, their already legendary Revolutionary hero, and of Governor John Hancock, of Declaration immortality. Adams was tepid; Hancock, aloof and cool, preferring to wait and see which way the political tides might flow.

After three weeks of heated debate a delegation headed by Adams climbed Beacon Hill to knock on the door of the wealthy and gouty Hancock. They proposed that the governor declare for ratification on condition that a series of amendments be tacked on for the consideration of the Congress.

The price for Hancock's support? The presidency, if Virginia failed to ratify or if Washington declined to serve. Otherwise, the vice presidency or, some say, the promise of Bowdoin's support in the next governor's race.

Hancock agreed to the bribe and, his feet swathed in bandages, was carried theatrically to the rostrum to make his "Conciliatory Proposition" as though it were his own brainchild. Adams, still the darling of both sides, seconded the resolution to consider the amendments, and a few days later added several of his own.

The Constitution carried on February 6, 187 to 168, making Massachusetts the sixth state to ratify. Considering that certain small towns, normally Anti-Federalist, were denied delegates because they were in arrears to the state treasury, and that a swing of ten votes would have brought defeat, and that the law of the land could not have carried without approval of populous Massachusetts, it can properly be said that the good ship *Constitution* almost floundered off Plymouth Rock before it ever got out of the harbor.

If John Hancock were indeed promised the vice presidency in return for his support, he was the victim of the first political double-cross in the history of the new nation.

But the "Massachusetts formula"—the idea of suggesting amendments along with ratification—became the vehicle which was to carry the Constitution past some difficult roadblocks.

Maryland

Maryland became the seventh state to ratify despite the harangues of Luther Martin and the doubts of Samuel Chase. Federalists dominated the convention, which first met at Annapolis on April 21. Following the example set by Massachusetts, a series of amendments, finally whittled down to thirteen, were suggested, but no formal action of approval or disapproval was taken. The vote to ratify was 63 to 11, on April 28.

South Carolina

South Carolina, planter country, became number eight on May 23, approving by a vote of 149 to 73 with the support of John Rutledge and the powerful Pinckneys.

New Hampshire

New Hampshire was but one of several states that probably would not have ratified had there been one general election day on which no state knew how the sister states would vote. Shortly after the convention met on February 15, an unofficial sounding showed the Anti-Federalists commanded a majority of four votes over the Federalist forces from the coastal and Connecticut River areas.

After ten days of fruitless discussion, the delegates could only agree to disagree. Recessing until June 3 (a date later set back to June 17), they returned home to seek further instructions from their constituents. When the convention finally reconvened, Maryland and South Carolina had ratified and the option strings around New Hampshire's neck had tightened.

And still the vote was close! On June 21, 1788, at 1 P.M., little New Hampshire, by the margin of 57 to 47, sneaked into the federal bosom, having absolutely no place else to go. Before the first toast was drunk, the clerk carefully noted the hour of ratification so that history would know whether New Hampshire or Virginia would have the honor of being the ninth and "clincher" state.

Virginia

Virginia, of course, did not make up its mind until four days later and then came perilously close to scuttling the entire ship of state. Virginia, largest state by far, sent a star-spangled cast of delegates to the convention that opened on June 2.

Patrick Henry, evangelistic in his opposition, dominated the proceedings to such an extent that his speeches took up more than one hundred of the six hundred pages of the official record, and the press referred to the Anti-Federalists as "Henryites." Others opposed were George Mason, Colonel William Grayson, Richard Henry Lee, James Monroe, and John Tyler, whose son was later to serve as tenth president.

The Federalist lineup was equally impressive: Edmund Pendleton, elected presiding officer, Chancellor Wythe, James Madison, John Marshall, and Light Horse Harry Lee. They were joined by the influential Governor Edmund Randolph who, though he had declined to become a signer at Philadelphia, jolted the Anti-Federalists and incurred the wrath of Patrick Henry when he declared that he could not obstruct progress by opposing ratification. The Federalists also worked with the comforting knowledge that the squire of Mount Vernon, George Washington, and the sage of Monticello, Thomas Jefferson, blessed their cause.

With this most distinguished cast, the largest and most important state staged the most impressive convention, the most statesmanlike debates, the clearest and most wide-ranging pronouncements of the rival philosophies of government. With both sides well organized and almost equal in strength, the sessions trumpeted on for more than three weeks while the fate of the nation hung in the balance. For if Virginia turned thumbs down, New York would certainly follow suit, and recalcitrant Rhode Island and North Carolina would have been only too happy to make it a foursome. Indeed, Governor Randolph received a letter from Governor Clinton of New York which virtually promised that if Virginia would reject, New York almost certainly would follow her example. But Randolph did not make the letter public until after the final vote had been taken. History can only conjecture what its effect might have been.

One of the most persistent Anti-Federalist arguments—one in which Thomas Jefferson sympathized philosophically from his minister's post in Paris—was the lack of a bill of rights. Again, the "Massachusetts formula" probably saved the day. It was agreed that a set of twenty-nine proposed amendments would be attached to the official report. With this concession, the crucial vote was taken on June 25 and ratification approved, 89 to 79. Consider that a change of six votes might have detoured the course of American history! The possibility of a United States where George Washington and Thomas Jefferson were regarded as aliens was dissipated.

New York

New York was an Anti-Federalist nest. And why not? From her strategic position commanding a great harbor and crucial waterways, she was able to impose heavy interstate tolls that virtually canceled the need for real estate taxes. The new government would strike down this windfall. It was no accident that the Anti-Federalist majority at the Poughkeepsie Convention was a solid 46 to 19.

Governor George Clinton and the two runaway delegates from the Philadelphia Convention, Lansing and Yates, joined with Melancton Smith, Thomas Tredwell, and Samuel Jones to lead the opposition. Their strength was clearly reflected when Clinton was chosen presiding officer. The affluent squirearchy of the Hudson Valley opened up their purses to defeat the new federal menace.

What happened in New York was also certain to influence the decision in North Carolina and Rhode Island, where the Constitution was equally unpopular.

Had the convention met in December or January, the Constitution could not have carried. But by July, the new law of the land was already a reality. Then came the knockout blow—news that Virginia had ratified. Cleverly, Alexander Hamilton posed still another threat to New Yorkers who pondered whether they could live outside the Constitution.

"Of course you realize," he told the convention, "that if you refuse to ratify then New York City will secede from the state and ratify by itself, and where will the Empire State be without its crown jewel?"

With seven grumpy Anti-Federalists abstaining, New York stamped a hesitant "OK" on July 26 by a vote of 30 to 27. There was nothing else to do.

Table 2   Ratification of the Constitution

State	Order of ratification	Date of ratification	Vote
Delaware	1	December 7, 1787	30–0 *
Pennsylvania	2	December 12,1787	46–23
New Jersey	3	December 18, 1787	38–0 *
Georgia	4	January 2, 1788	26–0 *
Connecticut	5	January 9, 1788	128–40
Massachusetts	6	February 6, 1788	187–168
Maryland	7	April 28, 1788	63–11
South Carolina	8	May 23, 1788	149–73
New Hampshire	9	June 21, 1788	57–47
Virginia	10	June 25, 1788	89–79
New York	11	July 26, 1788	30–27
North Carolina	12	November 21, 1788	194–77
Rhode Island	13	May 29, 1790	34–32

Source: Data taken from Richard B. Morris, ed., *Encyclopedia of American History.* Rev. ed. (New York: Harper & Row, 1961), and Clinton Rossiter, *1787 The Grand Convention* (New York: Macmillan, 1966).
*These votes were unanimous.

North Carolina

North Carolina, rural and reactionary, did not meet until the Fourth of July, by which time ten states were already in the federal barn and New York was trudging reluctantly toward the stable. Still, the farmer and frontier elements were skeptical. Technically, North Carolina did not reject outright, but *refused to ratify* until a lengthy list of proposed amendments could be assured. This action was taken on July 21, 184 to 83, whereupon the convention recessed. On November 21 North Carolina reconvened, reconsidered, 194 to 77, and sneaked in the back door.

Rhode Island

If North Carolina was "reluctant," Rhode Island was downright obstinate. The only state to refuse to call a ratifying convention stayed out in the pasture throughout the year 1789 and well into the following year. In the spring elections of 1790, the paper money adherents in the legislature suffered a setback. In the face of federal threats, the new state assembly quickly squeaked through a call for a convention, which approved the Constitution on May 29, 1790.

Rhode Island still did not enter graciously. The vote was 34 to 32.

While we cannot quarrel with the dictionary definition of an *enclave* as "a country . . . lying wholly within the boundaries of another," we prefer our own more realistic definition, "a body of land entirely surrounded by trouble." From the reassuring hindsight of two hundred years, it seems ludicrous to even think of tiny Rhode Island surrounded by a megapower United States on three sides and with a fourth side exposed to offshore attacks by predator submarines and battleships. Fortunately, the single switched vote that could have kept the state out of the Union was not forthcoming.

With Rhode Island sneaking in under the national wing, the thirteen sovereign states were truly *United* States as they set out "to form a more perfect Union, establish justice, insure domestic tranquility, provide for the common defense, promote the general welfare, and secure the blessings of liberty for ourselves and our posterity. . . ."

QUESTIONS

1. What was the name given those who favored the Constitution?
2. What practical political fact of life made it important to have the Constitution ratified by the people, rather than by members of the Confederation Congress?
3. How many states had to ratify the Constitution?
4. Did most citizens vote in the election?
5. Explain the ratification procedure.
6. Why did farmers generally oppose ratification?
7. How did the weather affect the vote for ratification?
8. Which state had the honor of being ninth to approve, thus assuring ratification?
9. What three states ratified quickly and unanimously?
10. Under what pen name did the three *Federalist Papers* authors write?
11. What important Virginia delegate declined to sign the Constitution, yet refused to join the Anti-Federalists?
12. Name the only state to grant general manhood suffrage for the vote on ratification.
13. Suppose you owned a small ship and transported goods along the seacoast and to the West Indies. Would you favor or oppose ratification?
14. Name the state that did not ratify until *after* the Constitution was in operation.
15. What official part did Thomas Jefferson play in the Constitutional Convention and ratification?
16. Why was Georgia so overwhelmingly in favor?
17. Who were the authors of *The Federalist Papers*?
18. Why was New York an Anti-Federalist nest?
19. What Federalist leader did most to convince New Yorkers to ratify?
20. What part did Patrick Henry play in the ratification process?

21. What was the key word that was on the mind of every delegate at Phila-delphia and every voter in the ratification process?
22. How did small states generally view the new union?
23. Why were the odds stacked against the Anti-Federalists?
24. What was the "Massachusetts formula"?
25. For awhile Virginia seemed ripe for rejection of the Constitution. If this had happened, what almost unimaginable situation would have occurred?

See Answers to Questions, pp. 171–72.

4

The Amending Process

Suppose you are offered a sleek new luxury car with all the trimmings, title free, with only one line of fine print reading: "Once the machine is driven off showroom floor, no adjustments or alterations may be made."

Great, if you yearn to be Queen-for-a-Day at the prom. Or King-of-the-Hill at the class picnic. Otherwise, your *limousine* can become a *lemonsine* overnight.

The most perfect constitutions are no better than finely tuned classic automobiles. They may require a carburetor adjustment as they climb from valleys to peaks. Or tire chains to keep moving in economic blizzards. Or bullet-proofing in terrorist terrain.

Without an effective method of amendment, a constitution's life can be as short-lived as that of a machine that cannot be serviced. Article V of the U.S. Constitution is a political safety valve, an instrument of change, a medium for growth, an emergency repair kit, a lifeboat attached to the governmental ship of state.

There are no amending articles in totalitarian countries. There is one alternative. They call it "revolution."

ARTICLE V—"FOR MANY ARE CALLED; BUT FEW ARE CHOSEN"

The U.S. Constitution handles change via Article V, the amending article. This chapter will discuss the American philosophy and method of change, then review the history of constitutional amendments. We shall also note the more

subtle methods which have transformed the original document: judicial interpretation, legislative hemstitching, presidential philosophy, and, most inexora-
ble of all, the gradual erosions and accumulations effected by custom, usage,
and by Father Time, who holds veto power in all governments and in all soci-
eties. At chapter's end the reader will find Questions plus a few tips on remembering the Amendments.

As the Founding Fathers labored over the process of orderly constitutional
change in sweltering Philadelphia, the country was still being governed by the
Articles of Confederation. Despite many faults, the Articles might have worked
if they had been amendable. But *the requirement that any amendment be
approved by Congress, then unanimously ratified by the thirteen colonies, had
been nearly fatal.* For instance, the Revolutionary War effort was crippled
when tiny Rhode Island refused to ratify an amendment empowering Congress
to impose an import duty. On another occasion, New York blocked an amendment designed to give the Confederation Congress temporary financial
power it desperately needed. The absurdity of requiring unanimous
approval was graphically illustrated even before the Articles came into effect.
Maryland did not agree to ratify the Articles until 1781—four years after
they had been proposed and two years after the other twelve colonies had
approved them.

To guard against such problems, our constitutional architects sought an
amending article that would be bendable but not trendable, tough but not insurmountable, responsive to genuine waves of popular desire, yet impervious
to self-serving compaigns of factional groups.

The Biblical saying, "For many are called but few are chosen," aptly de-
scribes the amending process finally adopted in Article V of the Constitution.
The scorecard tells the story of the few amendments that have survived. In the
first 197 years under the Constitution (through 1985), Congress considered
10,104 amendments and proposed thirty-three. Of these thirty-three, twenty-
six became amendments, and seven failed to be ratified.

These statistics become even more remarkable when one recalls that the first
ten amendments (the Bill of Rights) were mere formalities. The chances of an
amendment being proposed in the first 197 years were 306 to 1, and chances
of ratification were 390 to 1. But if the Bill of Rights amendments are excluded, the *real* odds against proposal today become 439 to 1 and odds against
ratification rise to 631 to 1. Once an amendment passes the proposal hurdle,
however, odds of eventual ratification are excellent: twenty-six chances out of
thirty-three overall; sixteen out of twenty-three if the Bill of Rights amendments are excluded.

METHOD OF AMENDMENT

There are two steps to the amending process: proposal and ratification. Each
step may be accomplished by one of two methods:

PROPOSAL

1. By a two-thirds vote of a quorum of both houses of Congress. (All twenty-six amendments to date have been proposed by this method.)

or

2. By a national convention assembled by Congress upon application by two-thirds of the states. (Never tried successfully; see below.)

RATIFICATION

1. By approval of three-fourths of the state legislatures. (Employed in twenty-five of the first twenty-six amendments; see below.)

2. By approval of specially called conventions in three-fourths of the states. (Used only once; see below.)

An amendment proposed by either method may be ratified by either method, thereby permitting four variations.

The alternate methods—number two in both instances—have been used so seldom that the author's students have suggested they were slipped in by professors just to make things more devious. The students certainly have a point, but the options were carefully examined by the Founding Fathers.

In the second method for proposal, the constitutional architects wanted a *method of circumventing the Congress*, of putting an instrument of change in the hands of the states and, indirectly, bringing the amending process closer to the people.

This method has been attempted, but has never succeeded. In the 1960s Senator Everett Dirksen (Rep., Ill.), irritated by the Supreme Court's one man, one vote decision in *Baker v. Carr*, proposed an amendment to allow states control over apportionment of state legislative districts. Dirksen chose the national convention approach and almost succeeded. By 1969, thirty-three legislatures (one short of the required two-thirds) had petitioned the Congress for a national convention. At this critical moment, one state rescinded its vote, and the momentum was permanently arrested.

As of 1987, the balanced-budget amendment was only two states short of the thirty-four necessary to petition Congress for a national convention.

The second method for ratification has been employed on only one occasion. Fearful of the pressure that might be exerted on state legislators by liquor interests, Congress chose the "special conventions in each state'" method for ratifying the Twenty-first Amendment, which washed out the Eighteenth (Prohibition) Amendment.

HOW CONGRESS HANDLES A SUGGESTED AMENDMENT

A bill to amend our Constitution is handled by Congress in much the same manner it would treat a bill to raise our taxes. It is referred to the proper committee, moves through various readings and printings, and differences in the versions passed by the House and Senate are compromised in joint conference.

The latest Equal Rights Amendment, for instance, was introduced and read in the House on January 3, 1985 by Representative Peter Rodino (Dem., N.J.), and referred on that day to the House Committee on the Judiciary. On March 6 it was referred to the subcommittee on Civil and Constitutional Rights.

The same amendment was also introduced in the Senate on January 3 by Senator Edward Kennedy (Dem., Mass.). It was read twice and referred to the Senate Committee on the Judiciary that same day. On May 13 the amendment was referred to the Subcommittee on the Constitution.

There are only two procedural differences between an amendment bill and other bills. An amendment must be passed by a two-thirds vote rather than by a simple majority; and unlike other bills passed by Congress, an amendment is *not* sent to the president for approval. Instead, it must be ratified by three-fourths of the states. Our present fifty-state union therefore requires passage by thirty-eight states.

Curiously, the president and vice-president of the United States and the state governors have *no official role in the amending process,* reflecting a centuries-old fear of the strong executive. They may, however, use the prestige of their offices and exert the leverage of their party leadership.

Historically, the Supreme Court has generally declined to make judgments about the politics of the amending process. This, in effect, makes Congress the arbiter. Congress has several times established that a state may turn down an amendment and later vote to approve. However, it would appear that a reversal of this procedure is not valid. Ohio and New Jersey ratified the Fourteenth Amendment, then passed resolutions rescinding their votes. Congress ignored the rescision, and the amendment, which needed both votes to pass, was declared ratified. In the early 1980s supporters petitioned the Court to make judgments on rescisions, but the deadline passed before the Court took action. It must be emphasized that Congress, in making decisions on amendments, is *not* bound by prior rulings. This is because it is the essence of Congress to be responsive to changes in public opinion.

FOUR AMENDMENTS THAT "OVERRULED" THE SUPREME COURT

Four times in American constitutional history Congress has passed an amendment to overturn decisions of the Supreme Court. The history of the Eleventh, Fourteenth, Sixteenth, and Twenty-sixth amendments spotlights an important link in the chain of checks and balances subtly built into the Constitution.

The Eleventh

When Chisholm sued Georgia in 1793 and the Supreme Court dropped a bombshell on states-righters by agreeing to hear the case, Anti-Federalists were outraged. (See comment on pp. 55–57.) Congress responded swiftly by proposing the Eleventh Amendment, which was ratified by the requisite three-fourths of the states within a year, though not *declared* ratified until 1798. The amendment protects states against suits by citizens of another state or of another country.

The Fourteenth

Congress and the High Court tangled again after the *Dred Scott v. Sanford* (sometimes spelled Dread Scott by abolitionists) case of 1857. Nine separate decisions were rendered on this case, but Chief Justice Roger B. Taney spoke for the "majority" in declaring that slaves could not be citizens and that Congress had exceeded its purview in prohibiting slavery in the territories. A Civil War and a few years of Reconstruction intervened before the Fourteenth Amendment, which conferred citizenship on all persons born or naturalized in the United States, could correct the Scott ruling.

The Sixteenth

Congress next "got around the Supreme Court" through passage of the Sixteenth Amendment, which legalized the income tax. In 1895 the Court turned down a federal income tax law on grounds that *the Constitution requires taxes to be apportioned among the states proportionately according to population.* But, in a spirit of cooperation, the Court *invited* Congress to overthrow the objection by means of an amendment. Congress proposed the Sixteenth Amendment in 1909 and the states ratified it in 1913.

The Twenty-sixth

President Richard Nixon, although signing a change in the Voting Rights Act that allowed eighteen-year-olds to vote in federal, state, and local elections, expressed doubt that the law was constitutional. Suit was speedily arranged, and the Court confirmed the president's misgivings in a 5–4 rejection that said, in effect: *"The Congress does not have jurisdiction over state and local elections."*

At a time when eighteen-year-olds were losing their lives in Viet Nam, the Twenty-sixth Amendment had wide popular approval. In record time it was proposed by Congress in March 1971 and ratified in June, giving eighteen-year-olds the right to vote in national, state, and local elections.

AMENDMENTS THAT FAILED TO "OVERTURN" SUPREME COURT DECISIONS

The number of Constitutional amendments designed to overcome a ruling of the Supreme Court would fill a Congressman's wastebasket.

The chronology of the Child Labor Law of 1916 and the Proposed Child Labor Amendment of 1924 offers an insight into the infighting that can take place between the legislative and judicial branches:

1916—Congress passes Child Labor Law, which prohibits interstate or foreign commerce of any goods produced in factories that employ children under age fourteen or in mines that employ children under age sixteen.

1918—Supreme Court declares Child Labor Law "unconstitutional," on the grounds that Congress' power over commerce does not apply because the *products* being produced by child laborers are not harmful, and regulation of child labor is a state right.

1919—Angry Congress, spurred by labor interests, passes new law exacting heavy tax on products of child labor, thus effectively barring such labor.

1922—Court strikes down 1919 act, ruling that *Congress has contravened the powers of the states*.

1924—Congress strikes again! Proposes Child Labor *amendment* giving Congress the right to regulate child labor.

1938—After fourteen years, during which twenty-eight states had ratified the proposed amendment (eight short of passage), Congress again enacts Child Labor Act.

1938—Happy ending! Supreme Court reviews third Child Labor Law within twenty years. Finds 1938 act constitutional, thus completely reversing itself. **Amendment unnecessary.**

Scarcely a month passes in which Congress does not consider amendments to circumvent Supreme Court decisions. Among those considered in recent times are efforts to reverse Court rulings on capital punishment, abortion, prayer in public schools, and reapportionment.

THE SEVEN THAT NEVER MADE IT

Ready for a little trivia? Okay. Name any two of the seven amendments proposed by Congress that failed to be ratified.

Well, the Equal Rights Amendment was one, you say. After that, the going gets rough. And rightly so, for the story of The Seven That Didn't Make It is a well kept secret in American political history.

It is a mere footnote to history that a package of *twelve*, not ten, amendments were proposed by Congress in 1789. Ten were ratified and became known as the Bill of Rights. Two others died and were buried in the *Congressional Record,* the daily log of House and Senate activity.

The following seven amendments were proposed by Congress, but failed to be ratified and never took effect (numbers one and two were in the original Bill of Rights):

1. The first would have empowered Congress to regulate the proportion of members of the House of Representatives once the proportion went beyond 100,000 persons per Representative.

2. The second might properly have been termed the "You-vote-your-self-a-raise,-you-better-be-ready-to-face-the-voters-before-you-receive-it" Amendment. It provided that "No law varying the compensation for the services of Senators and Representatives shall take effect until an election of Representatives shall have intervened." Sounds great! But what Congressman would ever vote for it?

3. This amendment, proposed in the second session of the 11th Congress, reflected a suspicion of all things royal dating back to Plymouth Rock. It would have stripped citizenship from anyone who "shall accept, claim, receive or retain any title of nobility or honour, or shall, without the consent of Congress, accept and retain any present pension, office or emolument of any kind whatever, from any emperor, king, prince or foreign power. . . ."

4. On March 2, 1861, two days before Abraham Lincoln's inauguration, proslavery forces gathered the votes to propose an amendment that would have "settled" the issue of slavery. It read: "No Amendment shall be made to the Constitution which will authorize or give to Congress the power to abolish or interfere, within any state, with the domestic institutions thereof, including that of persons held to labor or service by the laws of said State."

   Five weeks later, Union forces at Fort Sumter were fired upon, and a Civil War was under way over slavery, a domestic institution concerning persons held to labor or service by the laws of certain states.

5. The Child Labor Amendment was proposed June 2, 1924. It would have given Congress power to "limit, regulate, and prohibit the labor of persons under 18 years of age." Section 2 would have suspended any state laws that might contravene regulations established by Congress.

   Subsequent federal controls accepted by the Supreme Court, such as the Fair Labor Standards Act of 1938, have pretty much obviated the need for such an amendment. However, a retired top-ranking labor leader told the author in 1986 that President Ronald Reagan's proposal to establish a lowered minimum wage to help unskilled teen-agers obtain summer employment was "proof that a Child Labor Amendment is still needed."

6. The Equal Rights Amendment (ERA), stating that "equality of rights under the law shall not be denied or abridged by the United States or by any State on account of sex," was proposed in March 1972. A seven-year deadline was given an unprecedented three-year extension. That deadline expired in 1982. For details, see below.

7. An amendment to give the District of Columbia representation in Congress was proposed by Congress in 1978. It read: "For purposes of representation in the Congress, election of the President and Vice President, and Article V of this Constitution, the District [of Columbia] . . . shall be treated as though it were a State."

   The amendment also would have obviated the Twenty-third Amendment, which gave D.C. residents the right to vote in presidential elections. The measure expired August 22, 1985.

It is interesting to note that the setting of time limits for ratification was only begun in the twentieth century, and then only as an option of the Congress. Thus, a few of the above amendments are technically alive. For instance, the proposed Child Labor Amendment, which was ratified by twenty-four states, could properly be revived. Congress, however, would likely throw out the old ratifications because of the long passage of time.

The History of the Equal Rights Amendment

Abigail Adams wrote to the president of the United States, "Whilst you are proclaiming peace and good will to men, emancipating all nations, you insist on retaining absolute power over wives. Remember the ladies and be more generous . . . to them than your ancestors."

Crusty John Adams paid no more attention to this wifely advice than did his ancestors—or his Oval Office successors. From colonial times common law dictated a husband's control over his wife's person and property. Women could take no formal part in government, nor testify in court, nor serve on juries, nor enter the professions in a society where the superiority of men was deemed necessary because of supposed female intellectual and physical inferiority.

Slaves won the vote in 1869, but women were not enfranchised for another half century. The Nineteenth Amendment, granting women's suffrage in 1920, was the crown jewel in the showcase of female emancipation. Three years later, the first Equal Rights Amendment was introduced in Congress, where it languished. It was reintroduced in every Congress until 1972, with similar results.

But in 1972, the time was ripe. Congress proposed the amendment by the requisite two-thirds majority, thus sending it to the legislatures of fifty states for passage by thirty-eight states within seven years. Dramatically, Hawaii ratified *within two hours*. Within a year, thirty states had approved. With six years to go and only eight votes needed, the champagne was all but ordered and iced.

Between 1973 and 1977 five more states approved, but five others rescinded. With the proposition still eight votes short and time running out, Congress in 1978 granted an unprecedented thirty-nine-month extension—an action some constitutionalists termed "a dangerous precedent," and which Phyllis Schlafly, head of the highly effective Stop-ERA, called "changing the rules after the ball game has started."

But even with three extra "innings," victory never came about. Here are the statistics of a remarkable reversal of political form: With thirty-two ratifications in the first two years, only three more were gained in the last eight. *Not a single state ratified in the final five years.*

How could such a mighty crusade have been derailed? Let us count the ways: confusion of issues, doubtful strategy, shrewd opposition, and rigid constitutional safeguards.

The ERA scorecard pitted the powerful National Organization of Women (NOW) against Schlafly's Stop-ERA. President Reagan and various conservative organizations cheered for the Schlaflys. The influential League of Women Voters (LWV) and scores of activist groups worked independently or with established forces. Corporate interests, wary of ERA's economic impact, quietly pulled out their checkbooks to support the opposition.

Because many ERA supporters favored the pro-choice (abortion) movement, untold numbers of pro-lifers, particularly Catholics, were alienated. In the public mind, too, equal rights was sometimes associated with gay rights. Mrs. Schlafly capitalized by bringing up the specter of unisex toilets, government funding for abortion, homosexual marriages, and the drafting of young women into combat service. She called the opposition "a bunch of anti-family radicals and lesbians."

Some ERA supporters took drastic measures to win their cause. Feverish activity in Illinois, the only northern industrial state not to ratify, was not typical of the campaigns in other states. Nevertheless, the intense media coverage made it appear so in the public mind. Consider:

An overzealous activist was convicted of attempting to bribe a legislator.

Seven feminists staged a thirty-seven-day hunger strike in May/June 1982. *Time* (June 12, 1982) commented: "ERA foes have munched candy bars in the fasters' presence, and bumper stickers appeared with the message THEY NEEDED TO LOSE WEIGHT ANYWAY."

Seventeen women symbolically chained themselves to a brass railing in front of the senate office building in Springfield. After several days police, declaring a public nuisance, cut the chains and carried the women away.

Feminists smeared plastic bags with names of ERA foes, filled the bags with animal blood and tossed them outside the capitol. An angry and embarrassed Governor James Thompson likened the act to "painting swastikas on synagogues."

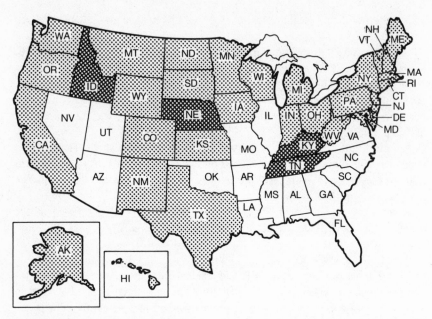

The Equal Rights Amendment was proposed by Congress in 1972. To be added to the Constitution, the proposed amendment needed the approval of 38 states. By early in 1977, 35 legislatures had ratified ERA (shown as shaded on the map), although 4 legislatures later rescinded their approval (shown as darker shade on the map). No states ratified after 1977, although Congress gave them an opportunity to do so by extending the deadline from March 1979 to June 1982. Having failed to get ratification, proponents of ERA plan to seek congressional approval again by initiating a new round of consideration by the states.

Despite these tactics the Illinois legislature voted in favor of the amendment by a simple majority. However, a variable legislative rule in force at the time required a 60 percent majority.

On the national front, NOW began a convention boycott of six states in 1977. Organizations across the country were urged not to hold conventions in Illinois, Florida, Missouri, Nevada, Georgia, and Louisiana. The tactic failed to gain a single ratification, but succeeded in alienating many businessmen and, ironically, thousands of women who made a living working at conventions in the target states.

But perhaps the most powerful deterrent to passage of any amendment is a creaky, yellowed document that will celebrate its 200th birthday in 1989. The Founding Fathers sought a Constitution that would be amendable, but not at a moment's notice. Their careful sets of checks and balances are either ingenious or diabolical, depending on one's political persuasion.

The requirement of a two-thirds majority of both houses of Congress immediately blocks hastily conceived or poorly backed propositions. And the necessary approval of 75 percent of the states assures that no mere parochial constitutional change could ever become law. But beyond this, the stipulation that *each state will, in effect, cast one vote* guarantees that every amendment must win broad geographic approval. This not-so-democratic clause gives Alaska (1980 population, 401,000) the same amending clout as California (23,600,000). It grants Utah and Idaho (2,400,00 combined) veto power over the eastern giants, New York and Pennsylvania (28,000,000). Other precious small-state warrantees occur in the impeachment process, the selection of a president when an election goes to the House of Representatives, and in equal senatorial representation.

Looking Back—and Looking Ahead

A victory in Illinois or Florida or Oklahoma might have triggered momentum for a late rally, but it was not to be. The first proposed ERA breathed its last on June 30, 1982, still three states short of ratification.

Proponents had reason to look through the tears with considerable satisfaction. After fifty years, Congress had finally proposed an Equal Rights Amendment. Seventy percent of the states had ratified. Opinion polls taken in ERA's last year of life showed that approximately 62 percent of Americans favored the amendment. A bit of luck in a key state or a Supreme Court ruling denying the right of states to rescind (time ran out before the Court acted) could have changed the score.

Opponents, of course, were jubilant. Phyllis Schlafly declared that ERA was "dead now and forever in this century." Questioned about her greatest contribution, she answered, "Making sure that eighteen-year-old girls would not be drafted." NOW's Eleanor Smeal, blaming "corporate interests," said her organization would be back as soon as "we've made a dent in the memberships of Congress and state legislatures." Kathy Wilson, president of the National Women's Political Caucus, was more specific. She singled out "the Dirty Dozen," twelve state legislators, ten of them Democrats, who rated the wrath of their constituents. Maureen Murphy, an Arizona Political Caucus spokeswoman, expressed confidence in ultimate victory, but told the author, "I hope the measure sits in Congress until we can isolate it from the irrelevant issues which proved deadly to the first proposed ERA."

Significantly, the identical measure was reintroduced in the first session of the new Congress in January 1983, and was labeled H.B. #1. Though the House rejected it in November, it is certain to be brought up again. Before the next crusade is completed, it will be up to the generation studying this book to examine the issues and choose up sides.

TIME—A SUBTLE AMENDER OF OUR CONSTITUTION

The U.S. Constitution is a blueprint for government, not an exhaustive rule book. At its birth, it penciled in a few boundaries. As it enters its bicentennial years, Congress and the American people are still filling in the details.

A Constitution, even if never amended, can no more remain the same than we can. Just as our habits, morals, and philosophies are colored by our shifting environment, affluence, and maturity, our Constitution is also in a state of flux.

In the late 1930s Clark Gable startled the movie world by looking Vivien Leigh in the eye and declaring, "Frankly, my dear, I don't give a damn." Twenty years later abortion and homosexuality were still whispered topics, AIDS was not even in the dictionary, four-letter words were unknown to movies, radio, or TV, unmarried couples carefully hid their liaisons, "house detectives" roamed hotel hallways to guard against visitations from the opposite sex, and drugs were not a widespread problem. Today, all that is changed.

Politicians who make laws, officials who enforce them, and judges who interpret them are products of the same society as the citizens they serve. Thus, the constitution is constantly, if subtly, being shaped, padded, and tinted ("amended," if you will) by the passage of time.

This is nowhere more apparent than in the issue of treatment of black Americans. At the time the Constitution was written, a black slave was considered to be mere "property," and was counted for the purposes of representation as three-fifths of a free person. The Supreme Court in *Dred Scott v. Sanford* (1857) continued this line of thought in its classification of black slaves as private property, subject for life to the dictates of their white masters.

Four years later (see "The seven that never made it"), we note that Congress supported the *Scott* decision. What other conclusion is there when Congress, by a two-thirds majority, proposed an amendment that would preclude an antislavery amendment or forever deny to Congress the power to abolish or interfere with slaves or slavery?

But after the Civil War ended in 1865, the Constitution was amended to repair the inequities over which the war had been waged. Within a period of five years, three "Civil War" amendments were adopted. The Thirteenth Amendment (1865) abolished slavery, the Fourteenth (1868) conferred citizenship upon all persons born or naturalized in the United States, and the Fifteenth (1870) secured black male suffrage.

Yet change was slow in coming. The decision in *Plessy v. Ferguson* (1896), approving "separate but equal" schools for blacks and whites, indicates that the High Court still viewed black Americans as second class citizens.

By 1954 Joe Louis had been a hero to Americans of all colors for twenty years; Jackie Robinson had opened major league doors for black baseball players. The armed forces had been integrated; blacks and whites had fought side by side in World War II. In this enlightened climate it was natural that the Court in *Brown v. Board of Education of Topeka* would say "separate but equal" schools were *not* equal.

The decision in *Plessy* in 1896 was 8–1; the reversal in *Brown* in 1954 was 9–0. Same schools, same issue, same Constitution, same Court—only different judges, different times. A classic example of the "amending" power of Father Time.

During the 1970s, the Court went further, upholding controversial affirmative action programs that favored blacks at the expense of whites. But ten years later, during Ronald Reagan's second term, the pendulum was beginning to swing to the other side. The courts were deciding cases of "reverse discrimination."

THE AMENDMENTS—TEXT AND COMMENTS

Now that we've discussed the amending process in depth, let's take a look at the amendments themselves and what they mean.

AMENDMENTS TO THE CONSTITUTION OF THE UNITED STATES*

The first ten Amendments were proposed on September 25, 1789 and were ratified on December 15, 1791. They are known as the Bill of Rights.

Amendment I

Freedom of Religion, of Speech, of the Press, and Right of Petition.   Congress shall make no law respecting an establishment of religion, or prohibiting the free exercise thereof; or abridging the freedom of speech, or of the press; or the right of the people peaceably to assemble, and to petition the Government for a redress of grievances.

Many words have been written and uncounted court cases have been adjudicated on the basis of these forty-five words. Yet these freedoms are not without their drawbacks. As *The Arizona Republic* put it: "The ... freedoms enjoyed by *The New York Times* ... protect ... the likes of *The National Enquirer*." He might have added, "and the American Nazi Party and the Ku Klux Klan." The same Supreme Court that told Gary Johnson it was all right to chant "America, red, white and blue, we spit on you," *(Texas v. Johnson, 1989)*, told Eichman that the First Amendment protected his right to burn the flag. *(Eichman v. U.S., 1990.)*

---

*Gray shaded areas represent the author's explanations and comments.

Subject headings, which do not appear in the original documents, are modifications of those to be found in *State of New Hampshire Manual for the General Court* (Concord, N.H., 1969), pp. 15–42. Spelling, punctuation, and capitalization have been modernized.

But First Amendment rights are not absolute, as Justice Oliver Wendell Holmes pointed out in declaring that *nobody* had the right to yell "Fire!" in a crowded theater.

In a more recent instance, the Court ruled that Matt Fraser's nominating speech for a fellow high school student, which was laced with sexual double meanings, was not protected by the Constitution. Former Chief Justice Warren Burger ruled that "it does not follow . . . that the same latitude [as is allowed adults] must be permitted to children in a public school . . . " (*Bethel School District v. Fraser*, 1986.)

The First Amendment does not protect an individual from the result caused by the liberties he has taken. Laws dealing with slander, libel, and misrepresentation provide for redress.

The first phrase reads "*Congress* shall make no law." As you read the first ten amendments, keep in mind that they apply to the *federal* government. Most of them have since been extended to the states.

Amendment II

Right of People to Bear Arms Not to Be Infringed. A well-regulated militia, being necessary to the security of a free State, the right of the people to keep and bear arms, shall not be infringed.

This amendment is a highly controversial one in a country that may be the murder capital of the world. The day before these lines were written, machine guns were advertised during the radio broadcast of a Chicago Bears football game. The National Rifle Association is lined up on one side of the issue, while law enforcement officials are generally in favor of abridgment of the right to keep and bear arms. Both factions have impressive statistics and arguments.

Amendment III

Quartering of Troops. No soldier shall, in time of peace be quartered in any house, without the consent of the owner, nor in time of war, but in a manner to be prescribed by law.

The practice of "quartering" soldiers in private homes was common in English history. Often, the promised remuneration was late, or reduced, or simply never paid at all. Frequently, the soldiers disrupted household activities; quite often the unwelcome visitors were rude, abusive, loud, and inconsiderate. The British continued this practice with the colonists in the eighteenth century, and the insult was remembered by the Founding Fathers in Philadelphia.

Amendment IV

Searches and Seizures. The right of the people to be secure in their persons, houses, papers, and effects against unreasonable searches and seizures, shall not be violated, and no warrants shall issue, but upon probable cause, supported by oath or affirmation, and particularly describing the place to be searched, and the persons or things to be seized.

What constitutes "unreasonable search and seizure"? Does the safety of our "person, houses, papers, and effects" apply to our glove compartment, the wastebasket in our hotel room, our garbage can, our telephone, our cassettes? May police, without a warrant, search a private junkyard for evidence of stolen goods? Does a regulation requiring certain customs officials to take urine tests to gain promotions violate constitutional safeguards? Does a school have the right to enter a locker it has rented to a student?

These are questions that have concerned U.S. courts, especially in recent years. How did some of these issues fare?

A federal judge ruled the urine test "shocks the conscience and offends this court's sense of justice."

The Supreme Court approved the search of Rudolph Abel's hotel wastebasket (*Abel v. U.S.*, 1960). By checking out of the hotel, the Court said Abel had abandoned the contents of the basket, and the proper owners of the hotel had given permission for the search. (Can we imply that the search would have been illegal if he had still been a resident?)

Amendment V

Trials for Crimes; Just Compensation for Private Property Taken for Public Use. No person shall be held to answer for a capital, or otherwise infamous crime, unless on a presentment or indictment of a Grand Jury, except in cases arising in the land or naval forces, or in the militia, when in actual service in time of war or public danger; nor shall any person be subject for the same offense to be twice put in jeopardy of life or limb; nor shall be compelled in any criminal case to be a witness against himself, nor be deprived of life, liberty, or property, without due process of law; nor shall private property be taken for public use, without just compensation.

Yes, there is more to the Fifth Amendment than the much-exploited privilege of remaining silent. Here are all the rights any suspect has a reason to demand. Of course, the terms "due process" (see the Fourteenth Amendment) and "just compensation" are subject to interpretation. The second clause is known as "double jeopardy."

Amendment VI

Civil Rights in Trials for Crime. In all criminal prosecutions, the accused shall enjoy the right to a speedy and public trial, by an impartial jury of the State and district wherein the crime shall have been committed, which district shall have been previously ascertained by law, and to be informed of the nature and cause of the accusation; to be confronted with the witnesses against him; to have compulsory process for obtaining witnesses in his favor, and to have the assistance of counsel for his defence.

What constitutes a "speedy trial"? Or an "impartial jury"? What kind of "assistance of counsel" is a defendant entitled to? For more on "assistance of counsel," see *Gideon v. Wainwright*, p. 111.

Amendment VII

Civil Rights in Civil Suits. In suits at common law, where the value in controversy shall exceed twenty dollars, the right of trial by jury shall be preserved, and no fact tried in a jury, shall be otherwise reexamined in any court of the United States, than according to the rules of the common law.

The twenty dollars is still applicable, uneroded by inflation. The Court has narrowed application, however. Six-person juries were allowed in *Colgrove v. Battin* (1973). And "suits at common law" no longer include numerous public rights that may not have existed in the ancient roots of common law. Nevertheless, sometimes even modern landlord-tenant actions have been covered by the twenty dollar umbrella of this amendment.

Amendment VIII

Excessive Bail, Fines and Punishments Prohibited. Excessive bail shall not be required, nor excessive fines imposed, nor cruel and unusual punishments inflicted.

Obviously, the meanings of the word "excessive" and the phrase "cruel and unusual punishments" may have different interpretations. An excellent subject for classroom discussion.

Amendment IX

Reserved Rights of People. The enumeration in the Constitution, of certain rights, shall not be construed to deny or disparage others retained by the people.

Puzzled? Well, so is the Supreme Court, which has said the "Ninth" contains "unenumerated and undiscovered" rights—a statement that would assure an "F" on your Constitution exam. The "Ninth" is partially the genesis of the disputed "right of privacy" mentioned in the *Griswold* (involving condoms) and *Roe* (abortion) cases.

Amendment X

Powers Not Delegated, Reserved to States and People. The powers not delegated to the United States by the Constitution, nor prohibited by it to the States, are reserved to the States respectively, or to the people.

The "Tenth" is the basis of an ongoing dispute between states-righters and supporters of a strong central government. Surely, Thomas Jefferson, a champion of states' rights, would be unhappy with today's skimpy leavings. (Especially in the interpretation of the Commerce Clause.)

Amendment XI

Proposed March 4, 1794, Ratified February 7, 1795.

Judicial Power of United States Not to Extend to Suits against a State. The judicial power of the United States shall not be construed to extend to any suit in law or equity, commenced or prosecuted against one of the United States by citizens of another State, or by citizens or subjects of any foreign state.

No other amendment is quite as mind-boggling as the eleventh, which prohibits an individual from suing a state in federal court.

When Chisholm successfully sued Georgia in 1793 in the Supreme Court, the rumblings were felt in every state house in the land.

"We told you so," screamed the Anti-Federalists.

"They've sold us down the river," moaned the advocates of state sovereignty.

When the Constitution was up for ratification in 1787 Federalists assured voters that state sovereignty would be jealously guarded. Although Article III, Section 2 provided that "the judicial power of the United States shall extend to controversies between an individual and a state," Federalists solemnly promised that this provision would not apply to suits against the state except in instances where the state would give its consent.

With *Chisholm v. Georgia* darkest fears became shining reality. Many saw the states as thirteen ducks blithely swimming on a federal pond that was surrounded by armed men lying in the blinds. And a 365-day hunting season was about to open!

It had all come about when Chisholm, a resident of South Carolina serving as executor for an English creditor, brought suit against Georgia for nonpayment of a bill. The Georgia state court refused to hear the case, claiming the state could not be sued. When no other court would accept jurisdiction, the U.S. Supreme Court elected to do so. Georgia lost the suit and the high court poured salt in the wounds by pontificating at length on the subject of state sovereignty. The assurances of the Federalists had become a litany of broken promises.

So instantaneous were the yelps that the wheels of the amending process began rolling the very next day in Congress. In less than a year Congress approved an amendment protecting the states against suits by citizens of another state, or by citizens of another country. The Eleventh Amendment was declared ratified by the states in 1798.

The Eleventh Amendment was emasculated by a devastating decision in 1908. In *ex parte Young* the high court ruled that the attorney general of Minnesota, in seeking to enforce a state act that is in violation of the federal Constitution is "stripped of his official or representative character and is subjected in his person to the consequences of his individual conduct."

A veteran lawyer who has tried cases on both coasts for thirty years told the writer:

> Article III, Section 2 clearly violated state sovereignty and invited Chisholm's suit. The eleventh is incomplete in failing to protect a state from a federal suit by one of its own citizens. However, there is always the refuge, *Forum Non Conveniens*—refusal to take jurisdiction because it is not convenient.

The eleventh could use updating. Suppose a New York citizen was injured at the Statue of Liberty Centennial and has a claim against New York and New Jersey. New York agrees to be sued, but only in its Court of Claims. But New York has no jurisdiction over New Jersey (and vice versa), while the Eleventh Amendment denies plaintiff access to federal courts.

Still, federal and state courts do a remarkable job of affording forums and remedies when police are negligent, or when a highway or flood control channel is improperly maintained, while preserving the sovereign state's immunity for its purely governmental functions. The system works, though not by the letter of the Eleventh Amendment.

The stipulation that a state may not be sued "without its consent" has been broadly and liberally interpreted in modern times as states have become increasingly sympathetic to claims against their responsibility. So liberal has this consent-to-be-sued trend become that an Arizona Superior Court judge gave the writer the perfect reason why the Eleventh Amendment restraint against suing a state in federal court is seldom a hardship.

"They [lawyers and plaintiffs] don't want to sue in federal court, anyway," he said. "The feds are much tougher on them than we [the state courts] are."

Amendment XII

Proposed December 9, 1803. Ratified June 15, 1804.

Mode of Electing President and Vice President.* The electors shall meet in their respective States and vote by ballot for President and Vice President, one of whom, at least, shall not be an inhabitant of the same state with themselves; they shall name in their ballots the person voted for as President, and in distinct ballots the person voted for as Vice President, and they shall make distinct lists of all persons voted for as President, and of all persons voted for as Vice President, and of the number of votes for each, which lists they shall sign and certify, and transmit sealed to the seat of the Government of the United States, directed to the President of the Senate; The President of the Senate shall, in the presence of the Senate and House of Representatives, open all the certificates and the votes shall then be counted; the person having the greatest number of votes for President, shall be the President, if such number be a

---

*This has been amended by the Twentieth and Twenty-fifth Amendments.

majority of the whole number of electors appointed; and if no person have such majority, then from the persons having the highest number not exceeding three on the list of those voted for as President, the House of Representatives shall choose immediately, by ballot, the President. But in choosing the President, the votes shall be taken by States, the representation from each State having one vote; a quorum for this purpose shall consist of a member or members from two-thirds of the states, and a majority of all the states shall be necessary to a choice. And if the House of Representatives shall not choose a President whenever the right of choice shall devolve upon them, before the fourth day of March next following, then the Vice President shall act as President, as in the case of the death or other constitutional disability of the President. The Person having the greatest number of votes as Vice President, shall be the Vice President, if such number be a majority of the whole number of electors appointed, and if no person have a majority, then from the two highest numbers on the list, the Senate shall choose the Vice President; a quorum for the purpose shall consist of two-thirds of the whole number of Senators and a majority of the whole number shall be necessary to a choice. But no person constitutionally ineligible to the office of President shall be eligible to that of Vice President of the United States.

The embarrassing election of 1800 showcases the necessity of an amending article that can rectify ambiguities or mistakes which the Founding Fathers failed to foresee.

Article II, in detailing the method of election of the president and vice-president, provided that the election be decided in the House whenever candidates for the two offices received the same number of votes. But when the Constitution was enacted the chance of a tie vote was considered to be remote. The Founders had failed to anticipate the rapid growth of powerful political parties. A hint of what was to develop cropped up in the election of 1796 when John Adams and C. C. Pinckney ran on the Federalist ticket against a Republican team of Thomas Jefferson and Aaron Burr. When the House met to cast ballots, Adams had the greatest number of votes. But party discipline and the rules of election were not sufficiently strong to give Pinckney the same number of votes as his running mate. As a result, Federalist Adams was named president and his long-time adversary, Republican Jefferson, became vice president. (Imagine a winning ticket of John Kennedy and Richard Nixon! Of Robert Dole and Rev. Jesse Jackson! Of George Bush and Geraldine Ferraro! Federalists and Republicans were both unhappy, but proposals for a correcting amendment were ignored until constitutional catastrophe was narrowly averted.

In 1800 the Republican candidate for president, Thomas Jefferson, and his vice-presidential running mate, Aaron Burr, each received seventy-three electoral college votes. (John Adams received sixty-five, C. C. Pinckney, Adams' running mate, received sixty-four, and John Jay received one.) The people clearly believed they had elected Jefferson president and Burr vice-president.

But Section 1 of Article II provided that "The Person having the greatest Number of Votes shall be the President, if such Number be a majority of the whole Number of Electors appointed; and if there be more than one who have such Majority, and have an equal Number of Votes, then the House of Representatives shall immediately choose by Ballot one of them for President;" The unscrupulous Burr conspired to take advantage of this constitutional ambiguity. Brazenly, he maneuvered to thwart the will of the voters and the intent of the Constitution by attempting to convince the House to name himself president and Jefferson vice-president. Only the intervention of Jefferson's political antagonist, Alexander Hamilton, who threw Federalist support to Jefferson on the thirty-sixth ballot, saved the country from the rule of President Burr.

The Twelfth Amendment, proposed in 1803 and ratified in 1804, provided that electors "shall name in their ballots the person voted for as President, and in distinct ballots the person voted for as vice-president." The electoral tragedy which almost occurred in 1800 would never happen again.

Amendment XIII

Proposed January 31, 1865. Ratified December 6, 1865.

Section 1

Slavery Prohibited. Neither slavery nor involuntary servitude, except as a punishment for crime whereof the party shall have been duly convicted, shall exist within the United States, or any place subject to their jurisdiction.

Section 2

Congress Given Power to Enforce This Article. Congress shall have power to enforce this article by appropriate legislation.

The Thirteenth Amendment was proposed in the waning days of the Civil War, after incalculable devastation had spread across the land. It is interesting to note how Great Britain's handling of the slavery issue differed from that of the United States. Although Great Britain's problem was never as acute as America's, she was involved in a lively slave trade and had thousands of slaves in her colonies, especially the West Indies. How did the British handle the situation?

The slave trade was abolished in 1807, and slavery was abolished by an Act of Parliament of 1834. The Act provided for a transition period during which slaves remained on the plantations as apprentices, owing part of their time to their masters. This gave both slaves and masters a few years to adjust before the slaves were set free. Parliament provided twenty million pounds as partial compensation to the slavemasters.

Should the United States have learned from Britain's example? Perhaps. Surely, from the clear viewpoint provided by hindsight, almost *any* financial settlement would have been a bargain when measured against the broken homes, the decades of bitterness, the vast areas of destruction, and the uncounted cost of mutilated bodies and lost lives. War is the only predator that skims off the cream of the crop.

Amendment XIV*

Proposed June 13, 1866. Ratified July 9, 1868.

Section 1

Citizenship Defined; Privileges of Citizens.   All persons born or naturalized in the United States, and subject to the jurisdiction thereof, are citizens of the United States, and subject to the jurisdiction thereof, are citizens of the United States and of the State wherein they reside. No State shall make or enforce any law which shall abridge the privileges or immunities of citizens of the United States; nor shall any State deprive any person of life, liberty, or property, without due process of law; nor deny to any person within its jurisdiction the equal protection of the laws.

Section 2

Apportionment of Representatives.   Representatives shall be apportioned among the several States according to their respective numbers, counting the whole number of persons in each State, excluding Indians not taxed. But when

---

*This amendment has been the basis of several far-reaching discrimination decisions of the Supreme Court, including *Brown v. Board of Education*.

the right to vote at any election for the choice of electors for President and Vice President of the United States, Representatives in Congress, the executive and judicial officers of a State, or the members of the Legislature thereof, is denied to any of the male inhabitants of such State, being twenty-one years of age, and citizens of the United States, or in any way abridged, except for participation in rebellion, or other crime, the basis of representation therein shall be reduced in the proportion which the number of such male citizens shall bear to the whole number of male citizens twenty-one years of age in such State.

Section 3

Disqualification for Office; Removal of Disability.   No person shall be a Senator or Representative in Congress, or elector of President and Vice President, or hold any office, civil or military, under the United States, or under any State, who, having previously taken an oath, as a member of Congress, or as an officer of the United States, or as a member of any State Legislature, or as an executive or judicial officer of any State, to support the Constitution of the United States, shall have engaged in insurrection or rebellion against the same, or given aid or comfort to the enemies thereof. But Congress may by a vote of two-thirds of each House, remove such disability.

Section 4

Public Debt Not to Be Questioned; Payment of Debts and Claims Incurred in Aid of Rebellion Forbidden.   The validity of the public debt of the United States authorized by law, including debts incurred for payment of pensions and bounties for services in suppressing insurrection or rebellion, shall not be questioned. But neither the United States nor any State shall assume or pay any debt or obligation incurred in aid of insurrection or rebellion against the United States, or any claim for the loss or emancipation of any slave; but all such debts, obligations and claims shall be held illegal and void.

Section 5

Congress Given Power to Enforce This Article.   The Congress shall have power to enforce, by appropriate legislation, the provisions of this article.

The most significant amendment of the century? Many experts would vote for the Fourteenth, which has been broadened considerably, especially by the Warren Court.

The Fourteenth protects against action of the states that unlawfully deprive a person of life, liberty, or property. This is the "due process," the "equal protection of the law," and the "privileges or immunities" amendment. Here we find the only attempt in the Constitution to define citizenship. That's right. There was *no* definition for seventy-nine years!

"Due process" has two branches: the *substantive* deals with basic freedoms that have been incorporated *by judicial decree* into the "liberty" protected by the Fourteenth Amendment.

It is also *procedural*, which concerns proper notice, an opportunity to be heard, to be defended by counsel, to confront accusers, etc. The right to a jury trial is guaranteed in criminal cases, but does not apply in civil cases.

"Equal protection of the laws" forbids any governmental action that *classifies individuals*—either for benefits or penalties. (Miami could not offer special public housing for Cubans; Utah could not extend tax breaks to Mormons.)

The "privileges and immunities" clause never took hold. Since the Slaughterhouse Cases of 1873, the clause protects nothing more than limited "national" rights of citizenship, such as the right to travel freely around the country.

The Supreme Court has made most of the freedoms of the Bill of Rights applicable to the states through the due process clause of the Fourteenth Amendment.

The first sentence of Section 4 made it constitutionally impossible for any coalition of southern congressmen to even suggest legislation prohibiting the U.S. from paying back money borrowed to wage the Civil War.

The second sentence prevented the federal government and the states from repaying funds borrowed to support the Confederacy. As a result, Confederate bonds and paper money became mementos, historical exhibits, wallpaper, bathroom tissue, and pipe lighters.

Designed for the Civil War, Section 4 is still in effect—a silent reminder to revolutionaries of the consequences of losing.

Amendment XV

Proposed February 28, 1869. Ratified February 3, 1870.

Section 1

Right of Certain Citizens to Vote Established. The right of citizens of the United States to vote shall not be denied or abridged by the United States or by any State, on account of race, color, or previous condition of servitude.

Section 2

Congress Given Power to Enforce This Article. The Congress shall have power to enforce this article by appropriate legislation.

While the Fifteenth Amendment gave former slaves the right to vote, blacks did not vote in large numbers until well into the twentieth century. In the South, literacy tests, grandfather clauses, poll taxes, registration difficulties, and white pressure held down black participation.

Although the three "Civil War amendments" (the thirteenth, fourteenth, and fifteenth) were passed primarily to give equality to newly freed slaves, their benefits applied to all. All people share the due process privileges of the Fourteenth Amendment.

Amendment XVI

Proposed July 2, 1909. Ratified February 3, 1913.

Taxes on Incomes. The Congress shall have power to lay and collect taxes on incomes, from whatever sources derived, without apportionment among the several States, and without regard to any census or enumeration.

No amendment ever affected the pocketbooks of Jane and John Citizen as profoundly as the sixteenth, which legalized the income tax. Adopted in 1913, it came as a counterattack on a Supreme Court decision of 1895, which ruled that a federal income tax violated the direct tax principles of two clauses of Article I.

The income tax slipped into the U.S. economy disguised as a lamb rather than the tiger it turned out to be. The first income tax law, passed in 1913, touched only one of every 271 citizens. A married man living with his wife received a personal exemption of four thousand dollars, a royal sum at the time, and then paid only 1 percent on *net* income up to fifty thousand dollars. Corporate net income taxes were set at 1 percent.

At one time lists of people who paid income taxes were posted on local post office bulletin boards. "Making" such a list was a genuine mark of affluence.

Amendment XVII

Proposed May 13, 1912. Ratified April 8, 1913.

Section 1

Election of United States Senators; Filling of Vacancies; Qualification of Electors.   The Senate of the United States will be composed of two Senators from each State, elected by the people thereof, for six years; and each Senator shall have one vote. The electors in each State shall have the qualifications requisite for electors of the most numerous branch of the State Legislatures.

Section 2

When vacancies happen in the representation of any State in the Senate, the executive authority of such State shall issue writs of election to fill such vacancies: Provided, that the legislature of any State may empower the Executive thereof to make temporary appointment until the people fill the vacancies by election as the Legislature may direct.

Section 3

This amendment shall not be so construed as to affect the election or term of any Senator chosen before it becomes valid as part of the Constitution.

For 124 years, U.S. senators were chosen by *state* legislatures. For instance, Illinois residents favoring Lincoln for U.S. Senator in 1858 voted for Republican *state* lawmakers; Douglas supporters voted for *state* representatives and senators.

This situation provided a constitutional set-up for an elite group of Robber Barons who brazenly "purchased the U.S. Senate" for a period of several decades prior to 1917. David Graham Phillips, in a 1906 "muckraking" series for Cosmopolitan, explains how simple it was to bribe a few poorly paid state legislators and thus control all legislation vital to the Baron's interests. Public outrage then brought on the 17th Amendment.

Amendment XVIII*

Proposed December 18, 1917. Ratified January 16, 1919.

Section 1

Liquors, for Beverage Purposes, Prohibited.   After one year from the ratification of this article the manufacture, sale, or transportation of intoxicating li-

---

*This amendment was repealed by the Twenty-first Amendment, effective December 5, 1933.

quors within, the importation thereof into, or the exportation thereof from the United States and all territory subject to the jurisdiction thereof for beverage purposes is hereby prohibited.

Section 2

Legislation to Enforce This Article. The Congress and the several States shall have concurrent power to enforce this article by appropriate legislation.

Section 3

Ratification. This article shall be inoperative unless it shall have been ratified as an amendment to the Constitution by the Legislatures of the several States, as provided in the Constitution within seven years from the date of the submission hereof to the States by the Congress.

The only attempt to employ the amending process to regulate people's social habits came about in 1919 with ratification of the Eighteenth Amendment. Prohibition proved to be a political disaster. It ushered in the era of gangsters, speakeasies, moonshine, and unprecedented violence. Many who disliked the taste of liquor began to drink, primarily because it was forbidden. From an economic standpoint, the cost of enforcement and the loss of tax revenue was heavy.

Millions of people drank toasts as number eighteen passed away, unlamented, in 1933.

Amendment XIX

Proposed June 4, 1919. Ratified August 18, 1920.

The Right of Citizens to Vote Shall Not Be Denied Because of Sex. 1. The right of citizens of the United States to vote shall not be denied or abridged by the United States or by any State on account of sex.

2. Congress shall have power to enforce this article by appropriate legislation.

The idea of women participating in government by voting was never seriously contemplated by the Founding Fathers. For 131 years, federal elections were controlled by adult males.

After the Civil War, when a campaign was launched to allow newly freed slaves to vote via a Fifteenth Amendment, suffragette leaders

Susan B. Anthony and Elizabeth Cady Stanton pleaded, "How about including women, too?"

But the suggestion was never seriously considered.

The Nineteenth Amendment, ratified in 1920, brought suffrage into the kitchen. For a couple of decades after that, husbands, fathers, and brothers did a reasonably good job of swinging the feminine vote in their families. But when Rosie the Riveter took off her apron and entered the defense industries in World War II, she began to do her own thinking. Rosie's daughters, active in today's feminist movement, have extended women's leverage in athletics, the pulpit, industry, and government.

Curiously, while the Constitution denied suffrage to women, it did not prohibit them from holding office. And prior to ratification of the Nineteenth Amendment, six states permitted women to vote in state and local elections. The constitutions of Wyoming (1890) and Utah (1896) brought the suffrage upon entrance to the Union. Referendums established the right in Colorado (1893), Idaho (1896), Washington (1910), and California (1911).

Neither Miss Anthony nor Mrs. Stanton, who battled for more than fifty years in the suffragette movement, lived to see their dreams fulfilled. Miss Anthony died in 1906, Mrs. Stanton in 1902.

Amendment XX

Proposed March 2, 1932. Ratified January 23, 1933.

Section 1

Terms of President, Vice President, Senators and Representatives.   The terms of the President and Vice President shall end at noon on the 20th day of January, and the terms of Senators and Representatives at noon on the 3d day of January, of the years in which such terms would have ended if this article had not been ratified; and the terms of their successors shall then begin.

Section 2

Time of Assembling Congress.   The Congress shall assemble at least once in every year, and such meeting shall begin at noon on the 3d day of January, unless they shall by law appoint a different day.

Section 3

Filling Vacancy in Office of President. If, at the time fixed for the beginning of the term of the President, the President elect shall have died, the Vice President elect shall become President. If a President shall not have been chosen before the time fixed for the beginning of his term, or if the President elect shall have failed to qualify, then the Vice President elect shall act as President until a President shall have qualified; and the Congress may by law provide for the case wherein neither a President elect nor a Vice President elect shall have qualified, declaring who shall then act as President, or the manner in which one who is to act shall be selected, and such person shall act accordingly until a President or Vice President shall have qualified.

Section 4

Power of Congress in Presidential Succession. The Congress may by law provide for the case of the death of any of the persons from whom the House of Representatives may choose a President whenever the right of choice shall have devolved upon them, and for the case of the death of any of the persons from whom the Senate may choose a Vice President whenever the right of choice shall have devolved upon them.

Section 5

Time of Taking Effect. Sections 1 and 2 shall take effect on the 15th day of October following the ratification of this article.

Section 6

Ratification. This article shall be inoperative unless it shall have been ratified as an amendment to the Constitution by the Legislatures of three-fourths of the several States within seven years from the date of its submission.

The record showed that federal officials defeated in November elections did not always show the same sense of responsibility and dedication to duty as they had when they knew their record would be subject to the scrutiny of the voters. Consequently, some highly questionable politicking occasionally took place between the time a so-called "lame duck" was defeated in early November and the time he left office on March 4.

It took the American political system—and the amending process—144 years to plug this constitutional loophole. The Twentieth Amendment clipped the "lame duck's" wings. It established January

3 as the date for the opening of the new Congress and moved the presidential inauguration up from March 4 to January 20.

The modern Congress is burdened with so many details that it is practically in session the year around. Thus the defeated congressman, in spite of the framers of the Twentieth Amendment, still has a short period in which to vote for legislation. The election recess and the Christmas recess further reduce even that period.

Amendment XXI

Proposed February 20, 1933. Ratified December 5, 1933.

Section 1

Repeal of Prohibition Amendment.   The eighteenth article of amendment to the Constitution of the United States is hereby repealed.

Section 2

Transportation of Intoxicating Liquors.   The transportation or importation into any State, Territory, or Possession of the United States for delivery or use therein of intoxicating liquors, in violation of the laws thereof, is hereby prohibited.

Section 3

Ratification.   This article shall be inoperative unless it shall have been ratified as an amendment to the Constitution by conventions in the several States, as provided in the Constitution, within seven years from the date of the submission hereof to the States by the Congress.

The Twenty-first Amendment recognized the hopelessness of the Eighteenth. The "noble experiment" was over after thirteen hectic years.

Amendment XXII

Proposed March 24, 1947. Ratified February 27, 1951.

Section 1

Terms of the Office of President.   No person shall be elected to the office of the President more than twice, and no person who has held the office of President, or acted as President, for more than two years of a term to which some other person was elected President shall be elected to the office of the President more than once. But this article shall not apply to any person holding the office of President when this article was proposed by the Congress, and shall not prevent any person who may be holding the office of President, or acting as President, during the term within which this article becomes operative from holding the office of President or acting as President during the remainder of such term.

Section 2

Ratification.   This article shall be inoperative unless it shall have been ratified as an amendment to the Constitution by the legislatures of three-fourths of the several States within seven years from the date of its submission to the States by the Congress.

Surprisingly, the Constitution fails to mention how many terms a president may serve. But George Washington, who could have had a third term for the asking in 1796, apparently settled that question for all time. Declining to run, he set an almost sacred two-term precedent that lasted 150 years.

In 1940 Americans were apprehensive about "changing horses in the middle of a stream"—that stream being World War II. They elected Franklin Roosevelt to a third term—then gave him a fourth in 1944. A number of prominent Democrats, led by Jim Farley, Roosevelt's campaign manager and Postmaster General, broke with the president on the third-term election.

The Twenty-second Amendment, limiting the presidency to two full terms, was proposed by a Republican Congress with some Democratic support in 1947, primarily to guard against "another Roosevelt." It was ratified in 1951.

Ironically, in the thirty-six years between ratification and the bicentennial of the Constitution, the only instance where a third term was a possibility concerned a Republican. The popular Dwight "Ike" Eisenhower, despite his seventy years and shaky health, might have kept the Republicans in power in 1960. But any such possibility was ruled out by the Twenty-second Amendment.

Amendment XXIII

Proposed June 16, 1960. Ratified March 29, 1961.

Section 1

District of Columbia.   The District constituting the seat of Government of the United States shall appoint in such manner as the Congress may direct:

A number of electors of President and Vice President equal to the whole number of Senators and Representatives in Congress to which the District would be entitled if it were a State, but in no event more than the least populous State; they shall be in addition to those appointed by the States, but they shall be considered, for the purposes of the election of President and Vice President, to be electors appointed by a State; and they shall meet in the District and perform such duties as provided by the twelfth article of amendment.

Section 2

Congress Given Power to Enforce This Article.   The Congress shall have power to enforce this article by appropriate legislation.

A common trivia question used to read something like, "I am a natural born citizen and permanent resident of the U.S., over twenty-one years of age, have never been convicted of a crime. Yet I am not permitted to vote for president or vice-president and am denied representation in Congress. What is my sin?

Answer: "Living in the District of Columbia."

For almost twelve years, New York and Philadelphia were the seats of government. When the capital was first moved to Washington, most inhabitants were residents of other states and considered the District a temporary home. They voted by absentee ballot.

As D.C. grew, hundreds of thousands became permanent residents. If they did not maintain a legal tie to a home in one of the states, they were disenfranchised in presidential elections.

The Twenty-third Amendment took care of that oversight.

Two hundred years after the Constitution was written, the District of Columbia is still not represented by a voting member of Congress. (A nonvoting observer sits in the House of Representatives.)

In 1978 Congress proposed an amendment whereby the District "shall be treated as though it were a State." The measure would also have wiped out the Twenty-third Amendment. Time ran out on August 22, 1986. Throw out the presidential/vice-presidential clause and the old trivia question and answer are still valid.

Amendment XXIV

Proposed August 27, 1962. Ratified January 23, 1964.

Section 1

Relating to the Qualifications of Electors. The rights of citizens of the United States to vote in any primary or other election for President or Vice President, for electors for President or Vice President, or for Senator or Representative in Congress, shall not be denied or abridged by the United States or any State by reason of failure to pay any poll tax or other tax.

Section 2

Congress Given Power to Enforce This Article. The Congress shall have power to enforce this article by appropriate legislation.

It may surprise today's college-age students to learn that it was necessary, as late as 1964, to pass a constitutional amendment to rule out the poll tax in federal elections. Yet at that time, Alabama, Mississippi, Texas, and Virginia still charged citizens for exercising their right to vote; and two states, Texas and Virginia, passed laws providing for "dual elections," which retained the poll tax in state and local elections. Today poll taxes at state and local levels no longer exist.

The six-month period at the beginning of the year 1964 was noteworthy for three historic "happenings" in the field of human rights. The Twenty-fourth Amendment was ratified January 23, the *Baker v. Carr* decision (p. 99) was handed down February 17, and on July 2 the most comprehensive Civil Rights Act in United States history became law.

Amendment XXV

Proposed January 6, 1965. Ratified February 23, 1967.

Section 1

Vice President to Become President. In case of the removal of the President from office or of his death or resignation, the Vice President shall become President.

Section 2

President to Nominate Vice President When Vacancy in Office of Vice President. Whenever there is a vacancy in the office of the Vice President, the President shall nominate a Vice President who shall take office upon confirmation by a majority vote of both houses of Congress.

Section 3

President Unable to Discharge Duties; Vice President to Be Acting President.
Whenever the President transmits to the President pro tempore of the Senate
and the Speaker of the House of Representatives his written declaration that
he is unable to discharge the powers and duties of his office, and until he
transmits to them a written declaration to the contrary, such powers and duties
shall be discharged by the Vice President as Acting President.

Section 4

President Unable to Discharge Duties: How Determined. Whenever the Vice
President and a majority of either of the principal officers of the executive
departments or of such other body as Congress may by law provide, transmit
to the President pro tempore of the Senate and the Speaker of the House of
Representatives their written declaration that the President is unable to discharge the powers and duties of his office, the Vice President shall immediately
assume the powers and duties of the office as Acting President.

Thereafter, when the President transmits to the President pro tempore of the
Senate and the Speaker of the House of Representatives his written declaration
that no inability exists, he shall resume the powers and duties of his office
unless the Vice President and a majority of either the principal officers of the
executive department or of such other body as Congress may by law provide,
transmit within four days to the President pro tempore of the Senate and the
Speaker of the House of Representatives their written declaration that the President is unable to discharge the powers and duties of his office. Thereupon
Congress shall decide the issue, assembling within forty-eight hours for that
purpose if not in session. If the Congress, within twenty-one days after receipt
of the latter written declaration, or, if Congress is not in session, within
twenty-one days after Congress is required to assemble, determines by two-
thirds vote of both Houses that the President is unable to discharge the powers
and duties of his office, the Vice President shall continue to discharge the same
as Acting President; otherwise, the President shall resume the powers and duties of his office.

What would happen to the country if, during a crisis, the president
would become physically or mentally unable to rule, yet refused to
yield his office?

A similar concern evolved around the vice-presidency, which was
left vacated for long periods of time when a change of office occurred
because of the chief executive's death.

The country had a preview of what might happen in 1919, when
President Wilson suffered a stroke. Several months of "petticoat rule"

took place as Mrs. Wilson virtually isolated the president. In the late 1950s, President Eisenhower was hospitalized after a heart attack. As in 1919, there were still no constitutional guidelines to handle or define the problem of incapacity.

The Twenty-fifth Amendment attempted to patch these constitutional weaknesses. Six years later it was put to use—not once, but three times within a period of twelve months!

On December 6, 1973, Gerald Ford was sworn in as vice-president, succeeding Spiro Agnew, who resigned.

On August 9, 1974, Vice-president Ford was sworn in as president, succeeding Richard Nixon, who resigned.

On December 19, 1974, Nelson Rockefeller was sworn in as vice-president.

Amendment XXVI

Proposed March 23, 1971. Ratified July 1, 1971.

Section 1

The Right of Citizens Eighteen Years of Age or Older to Vote. The right of citizens of the United States, who are eighteen years of age or older, to vote shall not be denied or abridged by the United States or by any State on account of age.

Section 2

Congress Given Power to Enforce This Article. The Congress shall have power to enforce this article by appropriate legislation.

Inflamed by the draft and a Vietnamese War they believed to be illegal, youthful rioters in the 1960s and early 1970s took to the streets. The smashed window, the slashed tire, the picket line, and unsightly graffiti became symbols of the day.

The period was highlighted by the march of a quarter of a million people on the nation's capitol in November 1969, and by the Kent State riot of May 4, 1970, during which four unarmed students were killed by National Guardsmen during a protest march.

The most insistent demand was the right of young people to vote. Even those who generally disagreed with the protesters saw the wisdom of the complaint that, "If we are old enough to be drafted and to fight and die for our country, we ought to be old enough to vote."

The Twenty-sixth Amendment was proposed by Congress in March 1971, and declared ratified by the states July 1. No other amendment was ever approved so swiftly!

STUDY TIPS FOR REMEMBERING THE AMENDMENTS

In the event you are asked to recall which amendment says what, here are a few study tips:

Attach one or two amendments each day to the refrigerator door and to bathroom walls and mirrors. Underline key words and phrases. Use highlighters.

Bring the dimension of sound into play. Recite essential information out loud. Discuss with friends. Make short tapes; play them frequently.

The following tips assume you understand the content of the amendments. The tips are intended to be *associations*; they are intended to trigger your mind, to marry the theme and the number in your memory. They are *not* complete. Some are a bit ridiculous, but in drawing associations, the more ridiculous the better. Personal associations are always best. You are urged to invent your own.

The First Ten

The Bill of Rights (first ten amendments) deals with basic freedoms and rights. One sentence may help you remember the first four:

"If we are to have freedom of expression and worship (1), we must have guns and a militia (2), composed of unquartered soldiers (3), who will protect us from unreasonable searches and seizures (4).

Also, think of 3 and 4 as "house" amendments: your HOUSE is free of quartered soldiers; your HOUSE (and person) is free from unreasonable search.

Numbers 5 through 8 deal with trials, courts, and imprisonment. Try this: "Even a gangster has a right to 'take the Fifth' (5), to have a speedy and proper trial (6), to a jury trial in important cases (7), and to reasonable bail (8)."

Another association: 8-ball and 8-bail. You'll be behind the 8-ball if you can't remember 8-bail. That might be cruel and unusual punishment.

And how thoughtful of the Founding Fathers to put the rights retained by the *people* (9), ahead of rights retained by the *states* (10).

That's it for the Bill of Rights. Remember this sequence:

Freedom of expression and the tools to defend it (1,2)

Two "house" amendments (3,4)
Four crime-related amendments (5,6,7,8)
And powers reserved for the people and the states (9,10)

Eleven through Twenty-six

Here are a few ideas to help you with the rest of the amendments.

Amendment 11.   STATE your own. (Concerns suits against states by citizens of other states or foreign states)

Amendment 12.   Twelve letters in T-O-M J-E-F-F-E-R-S-O-N, who almost had the presidency stolen from him for lack of a Twelfth Amendment.

The next three are Civil War amendments. They apply to *all* citizens, but were adopted especially to protect former slaves. Remember *the three "Ss"*:

Amendment 13.   Slavery (abolished).

Amendment 14.   Sitizenship ('skuse the spelling).

Amendment 15.   Suffrage.

INCOM(E)ING SENATORS DRINK WITH WOMEN

The simple sentence above contains the magic key to remembering amendments 16 through 19. A third grader can master them in an hour. Additional tips appear in parentheses.

Amendment 16.   Income tax. (Both siXteen and taX contain "X's")

Amendment 17.   Direct election of senators.

Amendment 18.   Prohibition (18 is the earliest legal drinking age in U.S.)

Amendment 19.   Women's suffrage.

Amendment 20.   Lame duck. In seeking to clip the lame duck's wings, the 20th moves the presidential inauguration up to January *20.*

Amendment 21.   Drowns out 18. Also remember that the two "drinking" amendments—18 and 21—have the same numbers as the minimum drinking age in most states.

Amendment 22.   Too-too-too easy! 22 and 2 presidential terms.

Amendment 23.   Rhymes with D.C.

Amendment 24.   Poll tax abolished. Only other tax amendment, 16, is also divisible by 8.

Amendment 25.   If veep or pres don't stay alive, look to number 25.

Amendment 26.   18-year-old vote. Since most of our readers are within a few years of their eighteenth birthday, we're sure they'll think of 26 as "last but not least."

QUESTIONS

1. What was the single fatal flaw in the Articles of Confederation?
2. Name the two official steps in the amending process.
3. Of these, which is the more difficult?
4. What are the two methods of proposal?
5. Has the national convention method ever been used successfully?
6. What official part do governors, vice-presidents and presidents play in the amendment process?
7. How are most amendments ratified?
8. What is the alternative method of ratification?
9. Has the alternate method been used?
10. Does Congress handle an amendment differently than it does a bill?
11. Can presidents, vice-presidents and governors act *unofficially* in the amendment process?
12. When a Supreme Court decision destroys a law passed by Congress, does Congress have any redress?
13. Which amendments were proposed to "overrule" the Supreme Court?
14. What was unusual about the time allotted for ratification of the Equal Rights Amendment?
15. What has the Supreme Court usually done when asked to review a political aspect of the amendment process?
16. Which amendment was put into effect in record time?
17. The Twelfth Amendment came about after the disputed election of which president?
18. The Eleventh Amendment came about because of outrage over which Supreme Court case?
19. How many amendments were in the original Bill of Rights package proposed by Congress?
20. Proposal by two-thirds of both houses of Congress is the major hurdle to eventual passage of an amendment. In the first two hundred years, how many *proposed* amendments failed?

The Bill of Rights; Which Amendment Am I?

_____ 1. I am the amendment which allows the individual states to form National Guards.

_____ 2. I provide citizens security against unreasonable search and seizure.

_____ 3. In criminal cases, I guarantee a "speedy and public trial by an impartial jury."

_____ 4. I make sure that certain basic, natural rights belong to every citizen, though they may not be specifically listed in the Constitution.

_____ 5. I guarantee a trial by jury in suits at common law where the amount in dispute exceeds $20.00.

_____ 6. I am the constitutional freedom cited by gangsters who wish to remain silent under courtroom interrogation.

_____ 7. I am the amendment cited by states-righters; I maintain that certain powers not specifically delegated to the federal government and not forbidden to the states *are reserved to the states*.

_____ 8. Because of me, Congress can "make no law abridging the freedom of speech, or of the press."

_____ 9. I prevent the government from forcibly quartering a soldier in a citizen's home.

_____ 10. I protect John Citizen against assessment of excessive bail, imposition of excessive fines, and from cruel and unusual imprisonment.

_____ 11. I provide basic constitutional rights for the citizen placed under arrest.

_____ 12. Thanks to me, the United States has no national religion, and every citizen is free to worship, or not to worship, without interference.

The Other Amendments; Which Amendment:

_____ 1. Might be said to have started women's lib?

_____ 2. Allowed citizens of the District of Columbia the right to vote for president?

_____ 3. Granted immunity to a state against suit in federal court by a citizen of another state?

_____ 4. Gave 18-year-olds the right to vote?

_____ 5. Brought about the direct election of Senators?

_____ 6. Provided for a new and orderly succession in the case of death, resignation or removal from office of the president or vice president?

_____ 7. Was the first of three "Civil War Amendments" dealing with slavery, citizenship and suffrage?

_____ 8. Was passed because Burr almost stole the presidency from Jefferson in the election of 1800?

_____ 9. Brought on the bootlegging era?

_____ 10. Ended the bootlegging era?

_____ 11. Insured that no voter will ever be charged a poll tax in a federal election?

_____ 12. Banned slavery in the U.S.?

_____ 13. Clipped the lame ducks' wings?

_____ 14. Assured that the right to vote may not be abridged because of race, color or previous condition of servitude?

_____ 15. Conferred a new type of *national* citizenship—quite apart from *state* citizenship—and conferred precious civil rights to all citizens?

_____ 16. Insured that no president will ever serve more than two *full* terms?

_____ 17. Legalized the income tax?

Fill in the Correct Anwswers

18. The _____ would succeed to the presidency in the event of the death of the president and vice president.

19. For more than a century Senators were elected by _____.

20. Prior to the _____ Amendment, a black slave was counted as three-fifths of a person for the purpose of legislative apportionment and direct taxation.

See Answers to Questions, pp. 172–73.

5

The Judiciary

THE MOST MYSTIFYING BRANCH

Among top Washington tourist attractions, the august and intimidating Supreme Court building, agleam with marble and brass, is perhaps the least known and the most consistently slighted.

The reasons are obvious: To the nonlawyer, the Judiciary is the most mystifying of the three branches of government. The black-robed jurists do not hit the front pages with the regularity of the headline grabbers who toil a block away under the capitol dome. They speak collectively ("The Court holds," "The Court fails to see"), appear to be unapproachable, avoid the prime time tube, and are not nearly as entertaining as the residents of the zoo.

This public neglect is most unfortunate, for the building, within whose walls are fashioned decisions which affect American life from crib to casket, offers a unique tourist treat: breathtaking design (the double, five-story, self-supporting spiral staircases are architectural masterpieces), excellent exhibits, a fine documentary film, and a continuing live demonstration of the world's most enduring and successful appellate performance. Even more impressive is the aura of hushed splendor that sinks into the soul of even the most irreverent visitor upon entering the great courtroom, where, in the words of former Chief Justice Warren Burger, "a whisper becomes a shout." Justice Burger was not referring to the superb acoustics, but to the Court's megatonic influence.

If the Judiciary is the least understood branch, the fault does not lie with the Founding Fathers. Though most were lawyers—and lawyers are known for their bewildering legalese—the Judicial Article is a model of simplicity. Its essence is contained in the first thirty words: "The judicial power of the United States shall be vested in one Supreme Court, and in such inferior courts as the Congress may from time to time ordain and establish."

All the rest is academic. Federal judges, if they behave (says Section 1) may serve for life at salaries that cannot be reduced. Section 2 broadly determines which cases fall within the federal judicial power. The previous Article (Article II, dealing with the executive authority) vested the president with the power to name all federal judges, subject to the advice and consent of the Senate.

How many Supreme Court judges shall there be? How much shall they be paid? What kind of "inferior" courts should be established? What qualifications must a judge have? Should they wear pink or white or green or black robes?

On these and dozens of other questions the Constitution is silent. Just as the chairman of the board leaves the annual picnic details—right down to the amount of mayonnaise in the potato salad—to the picnic committee, the Constitution delegates the judicial details to Congress.

Acutely aware that lack of a federal judiciary was a major deficiency of the Articles of Confederation, Congress responded by passing the Judiciary Act of 1789. The number of Supreme Court justices was set at six. Political infighting and expansion of the frontiers caused this number to vary between five and ten until 1869, when the present nine-member Court was established.

District and appellate courts were also established and have increased with population and territorial growth. Today there are eighty-six district courts and eleven appellate divisions.

Today's intricate federal court system is based substantially upon the simple provisions of Article III of the Constitution, implemented by the Ellsworth Judiciary Act of 1789, and occasionally modified by a piece of "growing pains" legislation.

CONGRESS AND THE SUPREME COURT

Congress enjoys several persuasive leverages in its give-and-take relationship with the Supreme Court. The Senate, through its power of confirmation, can control the personnel of the Court. Article III allows Congress to determine the size of the Court—a powerful weapon. If a vacancy is about to take place, Congress could reduce the number of justices. (Of course, the president could veto the measure, thus requiring a two-thirds vote of the Congress to override.) Likewise, Congress could add one or two justices, thereby shifting the philosophy of the Court.

Sometimes the mere hint of impeachment has an effect. Shortly after an inquiry into alleged conflict of interest was suggested, Mr. Justice Abe Fortas resigned from the Court in 1969.

It is conceivable that a vindictive Congress could reduce the Court's powers by requiring more than a simple majority of justices to override, or by lengthening or shortening the Court terms. (The Jeffersonians, always distrustful of the Judicial branch, postponed a term for an entire year.) Although Congress cannot lower Judicial salaries, it may refuse to raise them.

In Chapter 4 we noted that Congress can "overrule" the Supreme Court by proposing amendments to the Constitution. A less cumbersome and more frequently used maneuver is the passing of simple legislation that takes into consideration court objections to previous laws.

Historian Charles Warren traces the history of Congressional "reversal" of Supreme Court rulings to 1852 when the Court said that a bridge spanning the Ohio River must either be taken down or raised so ships could pass beneath. Congress replied by passing almost identical legislation, changing little more than a definition of commerce upon which the Court had made its ruling.

The justices then ruled, in *Pennsylvania v. Wheeling and Belmont Bridge Co.*, that the bridge *did not* interfere with interstate commerce, specifying that ships be refitted to permit passage under the bridge.

No finer example of Congressional "reversal" of Supreme Court decisions by legislation can be found than in the New Deal administration of the 1930s. In a short period the "Nine Old Men," as Franklin Roosevelt called them, fractured the Democrats' elaborate program to bring the nation out of the Great Depression. Their hatchet fell upon six of eight major New Deal pieces of legislation. Adjusting the phraseology to conform with Court objections—but leaving the content virtually untouched—FDR's wordsmiths "modified" the six butchered programs.

Five programs were sustained and a sixth went unchallenged! (See pp. 84–86 for details.)

THE PRESIDENT'S INFLUENCE

The decisions rendered by the Supreme Court and other federal courts are shaped by the personalities and predilections of the people who are chosen to sit on the bench. Through the power of appointment a president can therefore shape—or try to shape—the way in which the Constitution is interpreted.

By appointing the young, conservative intellectual, Antonin Scalia, to replace Warren Burger, a moderate, President Reagan balanced the Court's liberal/conservative alignment at 2–2—liberals Thurgood Marshall and William Brennan versus conservatives Scalia and William Rehnquist.

In the middle is a "swing quintet," four of whom are Republican-appointed justices. Justice Sandra O'Connor, a Reagan appointee, is considered a conservative, but has joined liberals on such issues as school prayer and liability of the press. She is "balanced" by Justice Harry Blackmun, tilting toward the liberal side. Justice Byron White, the only Democractic-appointee in the "quintet," and Justices Lewis Powell and John Paul Stevens are the least predictable.

It requires no crystal ball to predict that if Ronald Reagan's 1987 appointment of conservative Robert Bork were confirmed by the Senate, the president could shape American society well into the twenty-first century. Such a course would be even more certain if the justice replaced would be one of the two liberals, Brennan or Marshall, both of whom are over age seventy-five.

There are three reasons why things don't always work out as planned:

1. The Senate can refuse to confirm a key judicial appointment. Even the popular George Washington saw his nomination of John Rutledge for chief justice defeated. Recently, Richard Nixon's nominations of Clement Haynesworth, Jr., and G. Harold Carswell were rejected. Ronald Reagan's appointment elevating William Rehnquist to chief justice was subjected to sharp inquiry, particularly by Senator Edward Kennedy, on nationally televised Judiciary Committee hearings.

2. Because federal judges have the security and independence afforded by lifetime appointments, they often do not vote in the manner their presidential sponsors anticipated.

Reflecting on some of the Warren Court's liberal rulings, President Dwight Eisenhower called his appointment of Earl Warren "the biggest damn-fool mistake I ever made." Had he lived into the 1980s to review the thirty-year record of another of his appointees, the extreme liberal, William Brennan, the conservative Eisenhower might have called the Warren appointment "the *second* biggest mistake I ever made."

3. The third reason is illustrated by a happening in the life of Ronald Reagan. The president woke up Tuesday, November 4, 1986, with Republicans in control of the Senate, 53–47. By wake-up time Wednesday, the Democrats had gained a 55–45 majority. Now the opposition would have the chairmanship and majority membership on the important Judiciary Committee. In light of the delicate 5–4 Supreme Court balance, it suddenly appeared unlikely that *any* extreme conservative could now win Senate confirmation.

The voters had spoken. In the great political checks and balances tug-of-war, the ballot can be a most powerful weapon.

COMPOSITION OF THE SUPREME COURT*

Is the Supreme Court reasonably representative of the citizenry? Have the justices historically reflected the rich cultural and ethnic diversity of the Americans over whom they exercise pablum-to-pallbearer control?

---

*Statistics for this essay are taken from Henry J. Abraham, *The Judicial Process,* 3d ed. (Oxford University Press, 1975), with the addition of Justice O'Connor and Justice Scalia. Robert Bork's appointment is under consideration as this volume goes to press.

Not at all. Through 1986, 103 justices have worn the august robes. Color them white, Anglo-Saxon, Protestant, New Yorkish, native-born, and male. Despite the New York imbalance (fifteen justices were New York residents at time of appointment; twenty states have never had a representative), there has long been an effort for some geographical equity, possibly because it was simply good politics. Early in the nineteenth century presidents recognized the new states beyond the Appalachians by appointing midwesterners. And when the far west was being absorbed into the union, Abraham Lincoln specifically searched for, and appointed a conservative Californian, Stephen Field.

On another front, the statistics are startling: of 103 justices presiding through 1986, there have been only five Jews, eight Catholics, one black and one woman. These figures recall two political ironies. A southerner, Lyndon Johnson, appointed the first black, Thurgood Marshall, in 1967. And Ronald Reagan, who suffered withering political fire for his anti-ERA convictions, appointed the first female justice, Sandra Day O'Connor, in 1981.

NOTABLE PERIODS IN SUPREME COURT HISTORY

The Marshall Court

Just as a good parent influences a child's entire life, so did John Marshall shape the constitutional destiny of a young nation. Before he became chief justice of the United States, the Supreme Court was a weak institution that commanded little or no respect. The relationship among the judicial, legislative, and executive branches of the government was still uncertain, as was the relationship between the federal government and the states.

But after President John Adams appointed John Marshall to be chief justice in 1801, all that changed. During his tenure, Marshall shaped the Court into a powerful institution that was the equal of the other two branches of the federal government. Furthermore, his belief in a strong central government led to decisions that gave Congress far-reaching powers. He firmly established the notion of the supremacy of the federal government over the states in cases of conflict. Under Marshall's careful stewardship, the Constitution truly came to life as "the supreme law of the land."

It is no accident that historians, writing of the period from 1801 to 1835, use the words "John Marshall" and "Supreme Court" synonymously. Chief Justices have always believed that near-unanimous decisions are a healthy indication of Court strength. On at least five of his major opinions, Marshall's reasoning brought unanimous agreement.

One of Marshall's outstanding accomplishments was the establishment of the concept of judicial review—the power of the courts to declare laws unconstitutional. Today, we take this notion for granted, but it was Marshall who firmly enunciated the doctrine of judicial review in 1803 in the landmark case, *Marbury v. Madison*. (For details on this case, see p. 95.)

During his thirty-four years on the Court, Marshall lit many other constitutional beacons still glowing in the bicentennial years. In *Martin v. Hunter's Lessee* (1816), the Court exerted authority to overturn judgments of *state* courts that are not in harmony with federal law. This authority was extended to criminal proceedings of state courts in *Cohen v. Virginia* (1821). The doctrine of "implied powers" was enunciated in *McCulloch v. Maryland* (1819), where Marshall wrote "The power to tax is the power to destroy." The sanctity of the contract in America dates back to Marshall's opinions in *Fletcher v. Peck* (1810), and in *Trustees of Dartmouth College v. Woodward* (1819). The powerful *commerce clause*, giving Congress blank-check authority probably beyond anything envisioned by the Founding Fathers, was underlined by Marshall in *Gibbons v. Ogden* (1824).

A number of Marshall's most famous cases are discussed in detail in Chapter 7.

FDR AND THE SUPREME COURT

Franklin Roosevelt fully expected to inherit the Great Depression in 1933. But his confrontation two years later with the Four Horsemen came as a rude surprise.

When the president first set up housekeeping on Pennsylvania Avenue, the nation was still reeling from the Crash of '29. Thirteen million people were unemployed, more than nine thousand banks had failed. There was no Social Security, no unemployment insurance, and few pensions.

Where there was despair, Roosevelt offered hope. Working his friendly Democratic Congress overtime during the famous One Hundred Days, he turned out a comprehensive social and economic program aimed at "the three R's"—relief, recovery, and reform. Two days after taking office he declared a national bank holiday, then followed on March 9 by establishing the Federal Deposit Insurance Corporation to guarantee all federal bank deposits up to five thousand dollars. In record time he sponsored measures to raise wages, increase farm prices by limiting production, control the banks, put people to work on government projects, expand rural electrification, strengthen labor unions, bring order to the bituminous coal industry, create the Home Owners Loan Corporation and take the country off the gold standard.

Within two years, some of these measures were working smoothly; others were shaping up. That was when the Squire of Hyde Park came into classic confrontation with the Four Horsemen. Their names were Willis Van Devanter, James McReynolds, George Sutherland, and Pierce Butler—arch-conservative justices of the U.S. Supreme Court.

And what a traumatic experience it was! Picking up a fifth vote from moderates Owen Roberts or Charles Evans Hughes, the Horsemen trampled over the president's pet projects. The New Deal was rapidly becoming an Old Deal. Roosevelt, the positive thinker and supreme optimist, chafed under the judicial tyranny of "nine old men."

In his first term, Roosevelt had not made a single Supreme Court appointment. But in November 1936, voters gave him the largest plurality in presidential history. Flushed with new confidence, he made plans to strike back at the Court. In February 1937, he announced his court-packing plan. For every seventy-year-old federal judge who had served ten years, the president would be permitted to appoint an additional Supreme Court justice until the Court reached a maximum of fifteen. The same principle would be used for up to fifty appointments to lower courts. This would be one act of Congress the Supreme Court could not destroy, for Article III clearly left the composition of the federal judiciary to the discretion of Congress.

No president ever soothed the masses with the Pied Piper persuasiveness of Franklin Roosevelt. The magic of his radio voice was beamed to millions in Sunday evening "fireside chats," spreading the gospel of confidence and cheer and concern for humanity. "Every time he opens his mouth, it costs me a million votes," lamented Alfred Landon, his Republican opponent in 1936.

But not even a super-salesman could sell the court-packing plan. The Republican press called it "Machiavellian." Even fellow Democrats were skeptical. Disagreement brought about the first significant party split, sparked by the defection of Virginia Senator Carter Glass, "father" of the Federal Reserve System.

A funny thing happened while the Senate Judiciary Committee considered the bill in early 1937. Taking note of the Court's objections to the New Deal legislation, FDR's wordsmiths began to send the overturned bills through the Congress again, merely doctoring a few key clauses. (A primary Court objection was that Congress had unconstitutionally delegated too much power to the Executive.) Surprisingly, Justices Roberts and Hughes began to join Benjamin Cardoza, Louis Brandeis, and Harlan Stone in support of the New Deal. The first hint of a philosophical change came in March when a Washington State minimum wage for women was approved. In April the National Labor Relations Act was upheld, and in May a key provision of the Social Security Act was sustained. For the president, the old frustrating 4–5 defeats were magically becoming translated into glorious 5–4 victories!

Did Hughes and Roberts change their philosophy because of the new, conciliatory phraseology? Most legal historians doubt it. They think these two moderate justices sensed the long-range danger to the judicial branch if the proposed court-packing plan were adopted.

At any rate, the plan was unfavorably reported by the Judiciary Committee and later sent back ("buried" is a better term) to committee.

At this point the grim reaper and the rocking chair stepped in to accomplish what Congress refused to do: permit Roosevelt to pack the Court with men of the New Deal spirit. In June 1937, the seventy-eight-year-old Van Devanter resigned and was replaced by liberal Senator Hugo Black. The following year Justice Sutherland retired and was replaced by Stanley F. Reed; Frank Murphy came to the bench upon the death of Justice Butler in 1939; seventy-nine-year-old James McReynolds, last of the Four Horsemen, sensed the hopelessness of opposing the New Deal and resigned in 1941. He was replaced by James F. Byrnes, a conservative.

Two other jurists were also appointed during FDR's second term. William Douglas, a flaming First Amendment liberal, took the seat of Louis Brandeis, and Felix Frankfurter replaced Benjamin Cardozo. In all, Roosevelt made nine appointments, second only to Washington's ten.

In 1970 a panel of sixty-five law school deans and professors of political science, law, and history reviewed the records of ninety-six justices. Among the twelve rated "great" were Hughes, Brandeis, Stone, Cardozo, Black, and Frankfurter. Among fifteen "near great" were Sutherland, Douglas, Robert Jackson and Wiley Rutledge, all of whom served during the New Deal period. Even if the professorial panel was weighted toward the liberal side, it must be admitted that some great minds occupied the bench in the Roosevelt era. Referring to Justices Black and Frankfurter, Professor Henry Abraham said, "The two men towered over a Court with probably more talent than any other in the tribunal's history."*

Before Pearl Harbor, Roosevelt had a Court that reflected his own philosophy and would support him during the war years. A new liberal social philosophy would be encouraged in a Judicial Branch that had concentrated on property rights and the protection of business interests for a century and a half.

The Warren Court

Violent storms are preceded by menacing clouds, swirling winds, and bouncing barometric readings. Meteorologists cannot guarantee a storm, but it is easy to note when conditions are favorable.

So it was with the judicial upheaval that occurred in the United States in the period of the Warren Court, from 1953 to 1969. No one could be certain that it would take place, but any trained observer could have guessed that time and conditions were made to order for an explosion.

Consider these social and political factors:

The Supreme Court in the mid-1930s switched its focus from property to people.

By 1950 the army had been integrated. Jackie Robinson had broken baseball's color line. Government, management, and the working force were in the hands of people who had endured the most devastating depression and war in history. Unions were speaking up. Women were becoming assertive. Blacks were rest-

---

*Henry J. Abraham, *Justices and Presidents* (Oxford: Oxford University Press, 1974).

less. The Kinsey Reports brought sex out of the bedrooms and into the parlors and newspapers. Universities were bulging with veterans on the GI Bill of Rights, many of whom were fractious about time-consuming delays, waste, and inefficiency.

China had turned communist. The "Cold War" with Russia was on. The Alger Hiss Affair was still fresh in memory. McCarthyism was in its heyday. The intensely unpopular Korean War was drawing to a close after taking thirty-three thousand American lives. The United States had lost its nuclear monopoly.

In short, the world was uptight. *Everybody and his baby sister had suddenly discovered constitutional rights!*

In such an atmosphere Earl Warren became Chief Justice of the United States. The date was one to remember: September 30, 1953. During his sixteen-year tenure, the newspapers and an upstart newcomer to the media family—television—would make household words of such terms as Watts, Vietnam, Castro, Bay of Pigs, the U-2 Affair, abortion, the pill, pantyhose, latch-key children, NOW, Ms., single-parent families, school busing, day-care nurseries, Selma, homosexuality, Miranda cards, unmarried couples, integrated domitories, abortion, black power, pornography, "burn, baby, burn," and due process.

While TV cameras clicked, President John F. Kennedy would be assassinated. Before the decade was over, assassins would also kill the president's brother, Robert Kennedy; Malcolm X, leader of the Black Muslims; and Martin Luther King, undisputed leader of the black nonviolent movement. King's death would touch off waves of violence throughout the country, the most destructive being in Newark, Chicago, New York, and Detroit.

And a southerner, Lyndon B. Johnson, would guide the strong Civil Rights Act of 1964 through the Congress.

Earl Warren was a product of the liberal atmosphere of the Berkeley campus of the University of California. He practiced law for a few years, served as first lieutenant in the infantry, district attorney, attorney general of California, and won three consecutive four-year terms as governor. He was so popular with most factions that in 1938, when his name was placed on the Republican, Democratic, and Progressive Party tickets for Attorney General of California, he was top vote-getter on all three tickets! In 1948, when the Republicans sought to "balance" a ticket headed by Thomas E. Dewey, Warren was slated as a vice-presidential running mate. The move made no ideological sense, but it was an excellent balancing act. Dewey was starched and aloof, Warren was outgoing; Dewey was a New Yorker, Warren a Californian; Dewey was a conservative, Warren a liberal. Harry Truman gave them both a surprise.

Warren could not write as well as Cardozo or administer as well as Burger, his successor. He brought to the High Court not a great legal mind, but an open one. But as a Chief Justice, he fitted into the climate and the slot as neatly as though he had been appointed by the Muse of History. His forte was leadership. He could handle people. He was receptive to new styles, new ideas. Lawyers appearing before the Court found themselves involved in oral arguments as lively as any ever heard within the memory of long-time observers.

Court rules required four votes to review a case. Throughout his service, Warren always had Justices Hugo Black and William Douglas on his side when he wished to call up any case involving human rights. Justice William Brennan would join him in 1956, and Justices Thurgood Marshall, first black to be appointed, and Abe Fortas would be of help a little later. *As a result, the Warren Court probably agreed to accept more cases involving human rights than were heard in the previous 164 years.*

The Warren Court is best remembered for three blockbuster decisions in cases involving human values: *Brown v. Board of Education of Topeka, Baker v. Carr,* and *Miranda v. Arizona.*

In *Brown v. Board of Education of Topeka* (1954), the Court determined that black children in all-black schools—*even where all standards were "white"*—are deprived of equal educational opportunities.

The result? Forced busing. Increased taxes. Pockets of violent opposition. "Desegregation plans." Transfer of many children to private schools. Withholding of federal funds from districts that did not comply. A revolution in the way students would get to school, how and with whom they would study.

Considering the intensity of feelings on both extremes, it was fortunate that the decision had the force of unanimity.

In its second blockbuster case, the Warren Court took on inequitable legislative districting practices. Congress had always been glacially slow in adjusting legislative districts to conform with the flow of population. Historically, this imbalance enabled small towns and farming communities to exercise disproportionate control over many state legislatures.

The Warren Court struck at this inequity in *Baker v. Carr* (1962), with its famous "one man, one vote" decision giving federal courts jurisdiction in cases involving state legislative apportionment. In light of the mid-twentieth century mass movement from rural to urban areas and accelerated black voter registration, *Baker v. Carr* turned over enormous leverage to a new ruling class.

What *Brown v. Board* did for education and *Baker v. Carr* did for politics, *Miranda v. Arizona* (1966) did for law enforcement: it thoroughly shook up the powers that be. Here the Court introduced new guidelines to the term "due process."

The *Miranda* decision was foreshadowed by two years in *Escobedo v. Illinois* (1964), and applied to juvenile state proceedings in *In re Gault,* (1967). These and other rulings brought a new consciousness of constitutional rights to the accused and rewrote a basic chapter in the science of criminology.

In case after case, the Warren Court developed its own unique personality as it drove home its dedication to the Bill of Rights and the Fourteenth Amendment.

It declared that recitation of prayers violated the principle of separation of church and state. It narrowed grounds for search and seizure. It weakened the weapon of the libel suit and gave unprecedented license to the term "freedom of the press" by ruling that a public figure defamed by the media must prove actual malice to collect damages. It encouraged academic freedom. It was accused of "judicial creation" in "discovering" the "right of privacy" in a contraceptive case—a right found nowhere in the Constitution. This "discovery" would be picked up by the Burger Court in the celebrated abortion case, *Roe v. Wade* (1972).

In the first two hundred years of the Constitution, there never was a time when so many liberals sat on the Supreme Court as in this sixteen-year period when Justices Black, Douglas, Brennan, Fortas, and Thurgood Marshall at one time or another served under Chief Justice Warren.

In the bicentennial years, the jury is still out on the Warren Court. There is no question that many individual inequities occurred as the result of the school desegregation case. No one doubts that many patently guilty criminals have been allowed to walk the streets because of the *Miranda* guidelines. There will never be general agreement on this Court's constitutionally shaky venture into judicially created law.

One thing is certain: In any public assessment Earl Warren and his Court will draw proportionately more cheers from blacks than whites, from prisoners than prosecutors, from atheists than Christians, from "little guys" than giants, and from residents of Skid Row than of Park Avenue.

The Burger Court

Richard Nixon wanted to make it perfectly clear. When he took over the Oval Office in 1969 he promised to appoint judges who would *interpret* the law, not *make* it. He hoped that a transfusion of conservative blood would halt the liberal trend of the Warren Court.

The president soon had his chance. Despite rejection of two appointments, he was able to make four appointments in four years. The Warren Court became the Burger Court in 1969, when Warren Burger replaced Earl Warren as Chief Justice. Harry Blackmun came to the bench in 1970, and Lewis Powell and William Rehnquist joined in 1972. Burger was considered a conservative, Rehnquist an extreme right-winger; Powell and Blackmun were moderates.

But the Burger Court was never much of a counterrevolution.

Take, for instance the *Miranda* decision, which, law enforcement officials insisted, hampered their work. A few minor modifications turned out to be no big deal. *Miranda* held up remarkably well.

The Burger Court also supported its predecessor's one man, one vote principle, even to the point of throwing out a congressional districting scheme that had less than 1 percent variation between the most and least populous districts.

More dramatically, it extended Warren reapportionment principles to gerry-mandering. *Baker v. Carr* not only went unscarred, it was enhanced!

How did the Court handle "reverse discrimination"?

By neatly sidestepping it. The famous *Bakke* case of 1978 illustrates this maneuver.

Allan Bakke, a blond, crew-cut, thirty-eight-year-old student, charged that he was a victim of reverse discrimination admission policies by the University of California Davis School of Medicine. In an eagerly awaited and widely heralded decision the Court determined *that strict racial quotas are illegal, yet it is permissible to consider race as a factor*.

The *Bakke* opinion may be remembered for what it didn't do:

1. It didn't overturn affirmative action.
2. It didn't tell a generation of aspiring white professionals that they must postpone their education while centuries of injustices are being corrected.
3. It didn't completely please, or infuriate, anybody.

The case of *Wygant v. Jackson (Mich.) Board of Education* was another where an historic decision might have emerged. The Court found that the Board acted unconstitutionally in firing white teachers in order to preserve an affirmative action plan.

But the justices split so many ways and the decision was so involved that lower courts have had difficulty in interpreting it.

As a result, the Burger Court passed into history without flashing a definite red or green light on affirmative action. Many will argue, however, that the amber "Take it easy!" signs were exactly what the country needed, allowing precious time for tempers to cool and wrongs to be righted.

Freedom of the press.   What would be the Burger reaction to the revolutionary freedom of the press decision of the Warren Court in *New York Times v. Sullivan*? In that case the Court had ruled that a newspaper may not be punished for publishing false information about a public official unless it did so deliberately.

The *Times* appeared again before the temple of justice in 1971 for publishing the celebrated *Pentagon Papers*—secret Defense Department documents concerning the Viet Nam War. The Burger Court upheld the *Times* and the First Amendment freedom, holding the government had no right to enjoin publication. The decision was less than absolute, however, since it was based upon underhanded methods used by the government to obtain information.

Still, the Warren Court's 1964 decision on freedom of written expression remains intact in 1987.

Surely the most surprising decision of the seventeen-year Burger tenure came in *United States v. Nixon* (1974), when the Court said that in criminal

---

AN HISTORIC DECISION

The most historic decision of the Burger era had nothing to do with a case before the Court. It was made by President Ronald Reagan in 1981 when he appointed Sandra Day O'Connor to become the first woman justice of the U.S. Supreme Court.

Considered a conservative, Justice O'Connor in her first six years has displayed an independence of thought that has defied precise labeling. Shortly after the appointment the author was told by an official of the Maricopa County (Arizona) Superior Court, where O'Connor had served, that "She was the hardest working judge we ever had. Even when she finished a case after 3:30 P.M., she would immediately call for another."

The author has since had occasion to speak to a law professor who frequents the Court. Douglas Kmiec rates Justice O'Connor as "A skilled questioner whose opinions are well written and organized—and she'll sometimes surprise you. I think she surprises Reagan."

Apparently, Justice O'Connor has fitted neatly into the Court, philosophically and personality-wise. We applaud the appointment, not because it was politically shrewd, nor because it has greatly enhanced the women's movement, but because Sandra O'Connor may have been the very best available *person* to fill the job in 1981.

Which is a difficult admission for any male chauvinist.

---

cases a president—even the president who appointed four of its own members—may be subpoenaed to produce evidence. (Burger, Blackmun, and Powell voted against the president; Justice Rehnquist abstained because of a conflict of interest.)

Probably the most important case decided by the Burger Court was *Roe v. Wade* (1973), the abortion decision that touched off the charge of "judicially created law," and occasioned Mr. Justice Byron White's scathing observation about "an exercise of raw judicial power." (See discussion on p. 107.)

The Burger Court failed to develop a pattern or a personality. In the words of Columbia professor Vincent Alasi, it was steered by "rootless, activist, compromising moderation."

Notre Dame Law Professor Douglas Kmiec observed that "The Burger Court was incapable of a counterrevolution because it was incapable of achieving consensus on virtually any issue as indicated by the large number of plurality opinions and separate dissents."

Washington Post columnist George Will charged that "The Burger Court is responsible for the ruinous spread of forced busing as a 'remedy' for segregation . . . [and] misconstrued the 1964 Civil Rights Act to permit reverse discrimination . . . [and has done nothing] to reestablish the principle that government must be neutral between sects, not between religion and secularism."

The Rehnquist Court

The Burger Court became the Rehnquist Court in mid-1986, when William Rehnquist was moved to the Chief Justiceship, and Antonin Scalia took the seat vacated by Burger.

Looking at the Court from the position of an umpire situated behind the catcher, we note that the two extreme left-wingers, Justices Brennan and Marshall, are playing third base and left field, counterbalanced by the two strong right-wingers, Rehnquist and Scalia, at first base and right field.

The other "players," Powell, O'Connor, Blackmun, Stevens, and White, are stationed up the middle. Against certain batters (issues), a slight shift left or right can weight the defense. Blackmun figures to line up at shortstop with the left-wingers; White is likely to go to the right—say, at second base. Thus any change in attitude by any of the five, particularly O'Connor, Powell, or Stevens, would result in a 5–4 score.

It is obvious that any new player called in from the minors (lower courts) could swing Court policy. In October 1986, Manager Reagan had the power and popularity to control new players. But in November 1986, his Republican team lost control of the Senate and its Judiciary Committee, which have veto power over the manager's choice of players. A month later, Manager Reagan lost credibility because of the Iran-Nicaraguan arms deal.

Many doubt the Senate would approve an extreme conservative. Many feel there will be a Democratic manager in 1988. If a conservative is confirmed as successor to Justice Powell in the fall of 1987, many foresee a 5–4 swing.

What do you think?

THE COURT'S CLOUT

The Supreme Court has come a long way from the days of John Jay, its first chief justice. Today, when its gavel sounds, the reverberation is felt in every home and industry and institution in the land. The Court can tell people what movies they can see and what books they may read. It can prohibit prayer in public schools (*Engel v. Vitale*, 1962) or rule on whether a public school must accept students who are afflicted with AIDS. Perhaps the ultimate was reached in this land of freedom in 1942 when the Court, applying the commerce clause, told an Ohio farmer that he could not raise more than his government-mandated allotment of wheat even when every grain of that illegal wheat was consumed on the farm (*Wickard v. Filburn*).

In today's complex world the United States Constitution is, for better or for worse, whatever the Supreme Court says it is. And if the Supreme Court, in the words of Finley Peter Dunne's Mr. Dooley, "keeps one eye on th' illiction rayturns," maybe the man in the voter's booth has more clout than he thinks he has.

QUESTIONS

1. What courts does Article III of the Constitution establish?
2. What Congressional act established the federal judiciary?
3. Which president was particularly successful in circumventing Supreme Court decisions by altering legislation?
4. How many district courts and appellate divisions exist today.?
5. Who determines the number of justices on the Supreme Court?
6. What president postponed a Supreme Court term for an entire year?
7. Why was the Judiciary Act of 1789 considered so important?
8. How can a president exert major influence over the Supreme Court?
9. How may the president's power of appointment be weakened?
10. Who was the first black appointed to the Supreme Court?
11. What is judicial review?
12. Which chief justice established the power of judicial review?
13. Name two Supreme Court justices who reversed themselves during Franklin Roosevelt's presidency, thus turning 5–4 defeats into 5–4 victories.
14. How did the Supreme Court deal with Franklin Roosevelt's New Deal legislation?
15. How did Franklin Roosevelt respond to the Supreme Court's action?
16. Which president has made the most Supreme Court appointments?
17. How long did John Marshall serve as chief justice?
18. Which Supreme Court chief justice presided over the court at a time of great social upheaval?
19. What issue did the *Bakke* case consider?
20. Name three cases that are considered landmarks of the Warren Court.

See Answers to Questions, pp. 173–74.

Famous
Supreme Court Cases

The Constitution comes to life in the courtroom, where decisions may go far beyond the walls and influence the lives of millions of Americans. In this chapter, we'll take a look at how the Supreme Court has interpreted the Constitution in some of the most far-reaching legal decisions in American history. But first we'll take a moment to translate some "legalese."

THOSE BEWILDERING LEGAL CITATIONS

Brown v. Board of Education of Topeka, 347 U.S. 483 at 492–3 (1954)

Is the above citation bewildering to you? Actually, it is remarkably simple. The key to unlocking its precise meaning is one of the first lessons a freshman law student learns.

United States Reports, published by the U.S. Government Printing Office, has been the only *official* record of U.S. Supreme Court decisions since 1875. The citation above tells the researcher that the *Brown* decision may be found in Volume 347 of *United States Reports*, beginning on page 483; the quotation referred to is on pages 492 and 493; the decision was rendered in 1954.

Prior to 1875 the volumes of Supreme Court decisions were named after the Official Court Reporters (Dallas, Cranch, Wheaton, etc.) Cranch was the Official Court Reporter at the time of *Marbury v. Madison*. A citation from the first volume of Cranch would appear in the fifth volume of *United States Reports* and would read: *1 Cr. (5 U.S.)*

Because few nonlegal libraries carry *U.S. Reports*, and because few undergraduate students have occasion to research opinions not covered in their textbooks, this book does not include citations.

FEDERAL AND STATE POWERS

Judicial review: Marbury v. Madison *(1803)*

Section 13 of the Judiciary Act of 1789 provides that under certain circumstances a petitioner might ask the Supreme Court for a writ of mandamus (requiring an official to perform a specific act or duty).

Paragraph 2, Section 2 of Article III of the Constitution stipulated that except for certain special instances (cases affecting ambassadors, for example) the Supreme Court shall be limited to *appellate jurisdiction*. This meant that the Court would only hear cases upon appeal. Cases would not originate in the Supreme Court.

Take these seemingly innocent and unrelated clauses. Add the bitter Anti-Federalist court attitude of Thomas Jefferson and his Republicans, who came to power in 1801. Throw in a low-paying justice of the peace job that the Republicans did not want to give the outgoing Federalists. Turn these factors over to a courageous chief justice with a sense of historic timing, and you have the ingredients for the most famous case in American Constitutional history.

A day or two before leaving office, John Adams appointed forty-two men to justiceships of the peace in the Washington, D.C., area. The appointments were routinely confirmed by the Senate; the commissions were properly signed and sealed. *But the secretary of state neglected to deliver the commissions.* Suddenly, it was too late! Adams was out! A new breed of politicians was in!

Jefferson ordered his secretary of state, James Madison, to commission twenty-five of Adams' "midnight appointments," but to withhold seventeen. Among those denied jobs was a man named William Marbury and three genuine historical *et ceteras*: Dennis Ramsay, William Harper, and Robert Townsend Hooe. The four petitioned the Court for a writ of mandamus ordering Madison to deliver their commissions. (The thirteen others denied jobs did not even join in the suit.)

Chief Justice John Marshall routinely ordered Madison to show cause why the writ should not be awarded. But the Jeffersonians *canceled an entire year's session of the Court. Marbury v. Madison* simmered on the docket until 1803, by which time almost one-half of the period of the five-year terms had expired.

Marbury v. Madison can only be appreciated when viewed in historical perspective. The position of Supreme Court Justice was a demeaning one at the time. John Jay, the nation's first chief justice, resigned in disgust in 1795; Jefferson's cancelation of an entire session was a severe blow to Court prestige; a substantial section of the public was openly disrespectful.

As Marshall studied the *Marbury* case he was keenly aware of the recent impeachment of Judge John Pickering of the District Court of New Hampshire. On the state level, the Republican-dominated house in Pennsylvania had impeached Judge Alexander Addison. Now the Republicans were moving to impeach Justice Samuel Chase of the U.S. Supreme Court! The word was out: John Marshall would be next if he ordered Madison to deliver the commissions. Furthermore, Marshall realized he lacked the physical means to compel execution of the commissions. In the words of Jefferson's biographer, Albert Beveridge, "Jefferson would have denounced the illegality of such a decision and laughed at the Court's predicament."

The alternative—to admit that Jefferson need not comply—would be recognized as a sign of judicial weakness. The chief justice believed it would set a dangerous precedent for executive supremacy.

In handling the dilemma, Marshall satisfied neither Jefferson nor Marbury. Instead, he used the case as a springboard from which he would leap to judicial immortality.

Did William Marbury have a right to his commission? Yes, said Marbury in a lengthy essay.

If Marbury's rights were violated, does he have legal redress?

Of course, ruled Marshall. Wherever an inequity exists under the Constitution, a proper remedy must always be available.

Has Mr. Marbury taken the proper remedy in seeking a *mandamus* from the Supreme Court?

It was in his refreshingly original reply to this question that John Marshall shaped the course of American judicial history.

William Marbury, Marshall ruled, had no right to ask for a writ of mandamus, *for the Supreme Court is a Court of appellate jurisdiction, except for a few enumerated instances.*

If Section 13 of the Judiciary Act of 1789 allows Marbury to seek mandamus *in the Supreme Court, that section is patently opposed to the Spirit of Article III and is therefore unconstitutional.*

The important thing for the student to remember is that the Judiciary Act of 1789 *was an act of Congress*. Standing in the shadow of impeachment at a moment when the Supreme Court commanded neither public trust nor congressional respect, John Marshall established the Court as the umpire that would forever after declare "safe" or "out" on legislative actions of the Congress.

Judicial review—this power of the courts to rule on legislation—*is a uniquely American contribution to the science of government and jurisprudence.* It remained distinctly American for 140 years. Not until after World War II, when West Germany, Italy, and Japan also tried it, did any other government of any importance set up a similar system. (The Italian and Japanese experiments have not been successful.)

It is ironic that there is no mention of judicial review in the American Constitution. Alexander Hamilton thoroughly subscribed to the principle in *The*

Does a Supreme Court Justice have to be a lawyer? No.

Federalist. As precedents, several state courts had invalidated state legislation on constitutional grounds. In 1796 the U.S. Supreme Court, assuming the power to rule on acts of Congress, found a federal statute was in harmony with the Constitution (*Hylton v. U.S.*). But since nothing was upset, neither the decision nor the principle was widely noticed.

William Marbury never did get his job. There is no evidence that hundreds of thousands of students who have since studied "M & M" ever really cared. If any reader is looking for a bit of trivia to spring on an unsuspecting lawyer or history buff, ask for the name of the secretary of state who neglected to deliver the Marbury commission.

The answer, of course, is John Marshall! Truth has always been stranger than fiction. Nor would any fiction editor ever believe that Marshall and Jefferson were cousins.

The Contract Clause: Fletcher v. Peck *(1810)*

Your name is Robert Fletcher and you buy a tract of land from John Peck, who had obtained the property from the state of Georgia in the "Yazoo Land fraud." The Georgia legislature had passed the Act conveying the property.

When a new legislature passes a law revoking your deed, what do you do?

You sue Peck, of course. You have the good fortune of seeing your case wind up in a Supreme Court heavily influenced by Chief Justice John Marshall, a staunch defender of property rights.

The contract clause (Article I, Section 10) prohibits states, but not the federal government, from passing legislation that impairs the obligation of contracts previously drawn. The framers of the Constitution believed that such a provision, patterned after the Northwest Ordinance of 1787, was essential to a stable economy and the protection of property rights.

John Marshall subscribed to this gospel, and his thinking dominated the Court. The unanimous decision declared that Fletcher's contract was valid, *even though it was asserted that the law authorizing the conveyances was secured by fraud and outright bribery*. The opinion acknowledged that a state legislature may repeal an act of a former legislature, but held that when "a law is in its nature a contract, when absolute rights have vested under that contract, a repeal of the law cannot divest these rights."

Fletcher v. Peck is significant because it *extended the clause to contracts made with the state itself*. The case clearly foreshadowed the decision nine years later in *Dartmouth College v. Woodward*.

Sanctity of Contracts: Dartmouth College v. Woodward *(1819)*

A royal charter in 1769 established Dartmouth College as a religious college to be governed by a self-perpetuating board of trustees. In 1816 New Hampshire passed legislation to change the college to a state university. The original board was fired and a new one appointed by the governor. The original board brought suit against Woodward, the Dartmouth secretary-treasurer.

Chief Justice John Marshall ruled that the papers establishing Dartmouth were within the definition of a contract protected by the Constitution and that the contract was impaired by the state legislation. Since state legislatures were forbidden to pass any law impairing the obligation of contracts, this contract was "within the letter of the Constitution, and within the spirit also . . . ." He further found such legislative acts "repugnant to the Constitution . . . ."

Dartmouth v. Woodward became a classic case because of Marshall's precedent-setting opinion establishing the sanctity of the contract and for the eloquence of the attorney representing the original trustees, Daniel Webster. John Marshall's portrait deserves a special spot in every corporate board room.

Implied Powers: McCulloch v. Maryland *(1819)*

Article I, Section 8, p.18 of our Constitution cloaks Congress with the power "to make all laws which shall be necessary and proper for carrying into execution the foregoing powers and all other powers vested by this Constitution...."

In his opinion in *McCulloch v. Maryland*, Chief Justice John Marshall established this clause as the bountiful spring from which many of the broad powers of the federal government still flow.

The facts were simple: Congress established a national bank in 1816 and set up a branch in Baltimore. Maryland imposed a tax upon the bank, which cashier James McCulloch refused to pay. Suit was instituted, the Maryland state courts sustained the tax, and the case reached the U.S. Supreme Court in 1819.

The enumerated powers (Article I, Section 8) make no mention of a national bank. Marshall ruled that a genuine need for such a bank existed and that the "necessary and proper" clause applied.

"Let the end be legitimate," he declared, "let it be within the scope of the Constitution, and all means which are appropriate, which are plainly adapted to the end, which are not prohibited, but consistent with the letter and spirit of the Constitution, are constitutional."

Therefore, the Maryland tax was unconstitutional for, according to Marshall, "The power to tax is the power to destroy." These words are as familiar to law students today as the words of "Little Bo Peep" are familiar to nursery school pupils. Along with Marshall's equally known "Let the end be legitimate . . . ." quotation and the "necessary and proper clause," they have become the foundation for the doctrine of implied powers.

Strict constitutionalists have a pretty solid point when they quarrel with the "let the end be legitimate'" statement, for it certainly assumes a great deal. Under our system of limited federal powers, the Tenth Amendment reserves the balance of authority to the states. Marshall's analysis has been so solidly established, however, that the issue of authority is still often assumed.

The Commerce Clause: Gibbons v. Ogden *(1824)*

Three men well known to the pages of history are in the cast of characters involved in a case that established the importance of the"commerce clause," another source of vast powers of our federal government.

Robert Fulton, inventor of the steamboat, and Robert Livingston, who helped negotiate what has been described as "the world's greatest real estate bargain"—the Louisiana Purchase, were granted a monopoly to operate steamboats in New York waters between New York and New Jersey.

Fulton and Livingston in turn licensed Aaron Ogden, a former governor and former U.S. Senator from New Jersey, to run the steamboat operation. When Thomas Gibbons operated ships in competition, a New York state court granted Ogden an injunction prohibiting Gibbons from so doing. Gibbons appealed. The case wound up in the U.S. Supreme Court.

Chief Justice John Marshall denied the injunction.

In effect, Marshall's interpretation of the "commerce clause," granting Congress the power ". . . to regulate commerce with foreign nations, and among the states and with the Indian tribes," gave Congress a virtual blank check to control interstate commerce at the expense of the states. Today it is virtually impossible to think of any business that cannot be considered as being involved in interstate commerce.

States' righters were displeased at Marshall's ruling. But in the light of our modern automated economy, domination of commerce by the several states could become bewildering, chaotic, and, possibly, anarchical.

One Man, One Vote: Baker v. Carr *(1962)*

Suppose each school organization is allowed one vote on the student council. The Latin Club delegate, representing six Ciceroans, casts one ballot, and so does the delegate of the Marching Band, with 113 members. As a snare drummer, would you scream "malapportionment" if the Latins and the five-member Debating Club outvoted you, two to one, and you found yourself at the Roman Festival some crisp October afternoon instead of at the Homecoming Game?

Our case may be exaggerated, but in this land of equality, prior to 1962, some voters were far more equal than others. In Tennessee, for instance, the legislature had not redistricted itself in sixty years when a citizen named Baker brought suit against the Tennessee Secretary of State, Carr, charging he (Baker) was not receiving "equal protection of the laws" promised by the Fourteenth Amendment.

Until 1962 the Court had consistently adopted a "hands off" policy on apportionment, insisting that it was a *political* issue within the province of Congress.

Congress, in turn, was careless. In 1842 it prescribed that members of state Houses of Representatives must be elected from separate districts. Thirty years later it required all legislative districts to be approximately equal in representation; shortly after the turn of the century, the U.S. Congress further ruled that districts must be contiguous, compact, and as equal in population as practical. But enforcement was lax or nonexistent.

When legislation in 1929 omitted these restrictions, the Court gave its routine blessing. Thus, the *rules were no longer in effect*. Meanwhile, malapportionment became a creeping evil. The 1920 census, foreshadowing a trend, revealed that for the first time in history America had more city dwellers than farmers.

An Illinois resident, charging that one district had 800,000 more people than the smallest district, brought suit against the governor in 1946. Predictably, he lost. In the Baker case, it was charged that one Tennessee county with 2,300 voters was represented by one state representative, while another county with over 312,000 voters had only seven representatives. These are merely examples of the inconsistencies that were typical across the nation.

Then came the bomb! The Supreme Court announced reversal of a 173-year-old policy by ruling, 6–2, in *Baker v. Carr* that *distribution of seats in state legislatures is a proper issue for federal judicial supervision*!

John Joseph Citizen never heard the explosion, but the reverberations shattered the walls of complacency of every state capitol in the land. The revolution was on!

Application of *Baker* was speedy and effective. One year later Mr. Justice William O. Douglas enunciated the one man, one vote doctrine as the Court destroyed the Georgia County Unit system. In 1964 the Court extended *Baker* to include *both* houses of state legislatures (*Reynolds v. Sims*), and *federal congressional districts* were ordered to conform (*Wesberry v. Sanders*).

Coincidentally, the emergence of the black voter in the 1960s heightened the impact of *Baker v. Carr* even more. The Fifteenth Amendment, granting suffrage to the newly freed slaves in 1870, had been circumvented for a century in the deep South through such devices as the "white primary," literacy tests, grandfather clauses, the Ku Klux Klan, and the poll tax. Slowly, these devices disappeared in the twentieth century. The Twenty-fourth Amendment, knocking out the poll tax in federal elections in a few remaining states, was not ratified until 1964; two years later the Court ruled the amendment also *applied to state and local elections*.

Meanwhile, the 1965 Civil Rights Act and the 1965 Voting Rights Act provided the Justice Department with the weapons to enforce, including criminal penalties. Both acts were subsequently broadened several times. Today, millions of blacks have been added to the election rolls and black participation in the voting process is commonplace.

Together, *Baker v. Carr* and black participation have revolutionized the American voting process. Rural and small town domination of the democratic process has been uprooted by urban and suburban masters.

Executive Privilege: U.S. v. Nixon *(1974)*

Throughout most of our constitutional history, U.S. presidents and the Supreme Court maintained polite live-and-let-live relationships. In only a few instances did the Court touch such issues as presidential prerogatives and executive privilege. It stepped on Franklin Roosevelt's toes a bit in the 1930s; it told Harry Truman he could not take over the steel mills in 1952 even though he was commander in chief during the undeclared Korean War.

This Executive-Judicial love affair was shattered after a group of "plumbers" broke into Democratic national headquarters in the posh Watergate complex in 1972. The burglars were later identified with the Committee to Re-Elect the President. Their "loot"—information about the opposition— was as superfluous as a sprinkler during a deluge, for Richard Nixon defeated George McGovern a few months later by the largest plurality in history. It was the attempted cover-up of the operation, or "stonewalling," that aroused the media and the American people. A special prosecutor was appointed and revelation followed revelation. Many of the president's top aides were implicated and later went to jail.

When it was learned that the president had long routinely and secretly recorded Oval Office conversations, the Supreme Court subpoenaed certain of these tapes. Claiming that a president's constitutional duties would be jeopardized if his private papers could be opened to the public, President Nixon refused to submit the tapes.

Four of the president's appointees sat on the Court when the case of *U.S. v. Nixon* came up for review. Justice William Rehnquist disqualifed himself on grounds he had been an assistant to Attorney General John Mitchell, one of the Watergate defendants. The other three, Justices William Lewis Powell, Harry Blackmun, and Warren Burger, joined in the *unaminous 8–0 decision* ordering Nixon to turn over the tapes. While recognizing the principle of executive privilege, the Court ruled that it could not be employed to withhold evidence in criminal proceedings.

Few cases have had the sheer dramatic impact of *U.S. v. Nixon*. At home, the news monopolized the headlines and prime time TV. Friends of this author who were in Europe at the time insisted that Europeans were amazed that a Court, especially one containing three of the president's own appointees, could tell a president what to do.

The decision was announced July 24, 1974, at the time the House Judiciary Committee was holding public hearings on its impeachment inquiry. President Nixon turned over the tapes promptly and on August 9 became the first president to resign.

RIGHTS OF MINORITIES AND WOMEN

The "Peculiar Institution": Dred Scott v. Sanford (1857)

The All-Time Worst Decision in American Constitutional History, though difficult to digest, is better swallowed with a paragraph of historical background.

Article IV, Section 2 recognizes the institution of slavery. The Missouri Compromise of 1820 outlawed slavery in the vast Louisiana Territory north of 36° 30', except in the state of Missouri. The Fugitive Slave Act of 1850 denied trial by jury to slaves who escaped to free states. Congress passed the Kansas-Nebraska Act in 1854, permitting the people of these territories to choose whether to allow or prohibit slavery.

Dred Scott was a frail, illiterate slave who had been handed down in the Sanford family like a piece of furniture. In the mid-1850s, when he was approximately sixty years of age, suit was instituted on his behalf for his freedom on grounds he had lived with his master for five years in the Wisconsin Territory, where slavery was prohibited.

The fate of a nation hinged upon the *principle* involved.

Of the nine men in black robes who eventually sat in judgment on Dred Scott, seven were Democrats; five of these were from slave states. There were also one Republican and one Whig, both from the north.

The issues were clear:

1. Was Dred Scott a citizen of Missouri and thus entitled to bring suit in federal court?

2. Did Scott's residence on free soil entitle him to freedom?

3. Was the Missouri Compromise, making Wisconsin Territory free soil, constitutional?

The decision was rendered March 6, 1857, two days after James Buchanan was inaugurated. The Court's answer on the three questions were "No," "No," and "No."

1. Scott was a slave, said the Court, and could *never* be a citizen.

2. Scott's residence on free soil in no way changed his status, *for he was private property*.

3. Given these facts, the Missouri Compromise *had* to be unconstitutional.

Thus, for only the second time in history the Supreme Court had ruled an act of Congress unconstitutional. The first instance was in *Marbury v. Madison*, in 1803.

The Scott verdict was 7–2; all seven Democrats voted with the majority. Eighty-year-old Chief Justice Roger Taney, whose opinion was considered the "majority" one (actually, all nine justices filed separate opinions), unnecessarily irritated millions with such rhetoric as: (Negroes are) ". . . beings of an inferior order, and altogether unfit to associate with the white race, either in social or political relations; and so far inferior that they had no rights which the white man was bound to respect."

The consequences of the decision were profound:

The Democratic party was hopelessly split.

The brand new Republican party, which had entered the national political arena only five months previous to the decision, was almost assured a victory in 1860. Its candidate would be Abraham Lincoln.

With Congress constitutionally unable to handle the slavery problem, the alternative was Civil War.

Despite a Civil War and the Thirteenth, Fourteenth, and Fifteenth Amendments, the United States required a full century to even begin to heal the wounds.

Dred Scott, denied his freedom by the Supreme Court, was freed a few weeks after the decision by his master and died of tuberculosis on September 17, 1858.

Separate but Equal: Plessy v. Ferguson *(1897)*

"Our Constitution is color blind." You've heard that quotation many times. Have you ever wondered about the source?

To understand, one must go back to Homer Plessy, whose family tree contained seven great-grandparental white branches and one black branch. Still, in the 1890s in Louisiana, when the Ku Klux Klan and state "Jim Crow laws" were in their heyday, Plessy was considered "colored."

In setting up a constitutional case a citizens committee of Louisiana blacks hired a lawyer named Albion Tourgee. First step: Plessy purchased a ticket entitling him to a first-class ride from New Orleans to Covington, Louisiana, on the East Louisiana Railway.

Second step: Plessy made the calculated "mistake" of sitting in the first-class car reserved for whites. A conductor commanded him to move to the colored first-class coach.

Plessy refused and was arrested. Suit was brought against the railroad. Plessy contended that the Louisiana statute violated the equal protection clause of the Fourteenth Amendment. Judge John Ferguson ruled that the statute did not violate the equal protection clause.

The case reached the U.S. Supreme Court on a writ of error. The Court upheld Ferguson's decision. *Seven justices ruled that the Constitution never intended to put blacks and whites at the same level socially. It was sufficient, said the Court, that both races enjoy "separate but equal" civil rights.*

It is likely that the "color-blind" quotation was adapted from a sentence in Tourgee's peroration in which he said: "Justice is pictured as blind, and her daughter, the law, ought at least to be color blind."

The single ray of sunshine to emerge from the dark cloud of *Plessy* came in the dissent of a lone justice, John Marshall Harlan. His ringing minority opinion stands as one of the shining dissents in American constitutional history. Here are a few quotations:

> . . . there is . . . no superior, dominant ruling class of citizens. There is no caste here.

> In respect of civil rights, all citizens are equal before the law. The humblest is the peer of the most powerful.

> In my opinion, the judgment this day rendered will, in time, prove to be quite as pernicious as the decision . . . in the *Dred Scott* case.

> Sixty millions of whites are in no danger from the presence here of eight millions of blacks.

> The thin disguise of "equal" accommodations . . . will not mislead anyone, or atone for the wrong this day done.

The story-behind-the-story hits the reader only after he examines Mr. Justice Harlan's background:

His was a proud slave-holding Kentucky family.

When the Senate was considering Harlan's confirmation, a Union general wrote the committee that Harlan had told him during the war that: "He [Harlan] had no more conscientious scruples in buying and selling a Negro than he had in buying and selling a horse . . . and that the liberation of slaves by our general government was a direct violation of the Constitution . . . ."*

He joined the nativistic, xenophobic, anti-Catholic Know-Nothing Party in 1854.

He was elected City Attorney of Frankfort, Kentucky, with Know-Nothing support.

As a Whig candidate for Congress, he supported the *Dred Scott* decision, and lost by only fifty votes.

During the Civil War, he formed a regiment of Kentucky volunteers and was commissioned a colonel. He turned his troops over to Union General Thomas.

---

*Alan Westin. "John Marshall Harlan and the Constitutional Rights of Negroes: The Transformation of a Southerner," *Yale Law Journal* 66, no. 637, April 1957. Quoted from Alan Barth, *Prophets with Honor* (New York: Alfred A. Knopf, 1974).

However, he told his men he "would lead them over to the Confederate side if Lincoln and the Radical Republicans in Washington tried to abolish slavery."

He attacked Lincoln for the Emancipation Proclamation.

He opposed ratification of the Thirteenth Amendment (abolishing slavery) and the Fourteenth (civil rights).

Running for the governorship of Kentucky in 1871, he declared it was "right and proper" for public schools to keep "whites and blacks separate."

How does the student of history account for Harlan's 180-degree turnabout? Was it because his respect for the law won out over his deep-seated convictions? Was it because his oath of office was more sacred to him than family, friends, neighbors? History only records that it would be fifty-eight years before the Court, in *Brown v. Board of Education* (1954), would be enlightened enough to catch up with this "bigoted" justice.

School Desegregation: Brown v. Board of Education of Topeka *(1954)*

The doctrine of "separate but equal" first appeared in U.S. history books in 1850 with the Massachusetts Supreme Court ruling in *Roberts v. City of Boston*. The U. S. Supreme Court blessed the principle forty-six years later (see *Plessy v. Ferguson,* page 103). Despite its noble rhetoric, the Fourteenth Amendment of 1868 had little significance in this matter for ninety-six additional years.

Not until 1927 did the Taft Court face the issue—and deftly pass it off to the state legislatures (*Gong Lum v. Rice*).

Why was the Court ready to tackle *Brown* in 1954, yet unable to do so in 1896 or 1927? Probably because, in the words of Mr. Dooley again, the Court really does "kape one eye on th' iliction rayturns."

The road to *Brown* was constructed by massive migrations of southern blacks to northern industrial states beginning shortly before World War I; by hard-nosed votes-for-jobs political leverage at the precinct level; by World War II; by black enlistment and black union representation; and, in the postwar period, by the persistent and sometimes brilliant behind-the-scenes strategy of a little group of black lawyers working with the National Association for the Advancement of Colored People. And, oh yes, a new liberal Court that also kept an eye on changing times.

The NAACP game plan, beginning in the late 1930s, was to avoid the emotional trauma of walking black boys and girls through the grammar school door. Instead, black students were squeezed through the back doors of graduate professional schools. The reason: Establishing separate-but-*really*-equal facilities for a handful of graduate students is extremely difficult and prohibitively expensive. Here they found a sympathetic Supreme Court.

In 1938 the University of Missouri Law School turned down the application of a black, even though equal accommodations were not available. Though the university agreed to pay the student's expenses in a northern law school, the Court ruled Missouri's action was a violation of the equal protection clause of the Fourteenth Amendment (*Missouri ex rel. Gaines v. Canada*).

World War II stalled the campaign for several years, but in 1948 the University of Oklahoma was forced to realize that building equal facilities for blacks was too costly to contemplate. It agreed, following a ruling (*Sipuel v. Board of Regents of University of Oklahoma*) to admit blacks for any course not offered by its State College for Negroes.

Two years later the crusaders celebrated a double victory on the same day. Rather than admit a black, the University of Texas set up, in record time, a separate black law school. The student refused to enter; the Court then ordered the white University of Texas law school to enroll him. The precedent established remained long after the student flunked out.

That same day the decision was handed down in *McLaurin v. Oklahoma State Regents*. The University of Oklahoma College of Education, forced to admit a black student, roped him off from whites in the classroom, dining room, library, etc. The Court refused to allow this practice.

The little victories began to add up. A *Brown v. Board* confrontation was clearly in the future. And the appointment of Earl Warren to the Chief Justiceship in 1953 virtually assured the result.

In hearing the case against the Topeka Board of Education the Court lumped four similar cases (in South Carolina, Virginia, Delaware, and Kansas) into one package.

The arguments in the case centered around the historical meaning of the equal protection clause of the Fourteenth Amendment. Untold millions of students and their families are aware that the Court, in a unanimous decision, found that the plaintiffs had been deprived of "equal protection of the laws," guaranteed by the Fourteenth Amendment. The court opinion, written by Chief Justice Earl Warren, stated that segregation harms black children because it "generates a feeling of inferiority as to their status in the community that may affect their hearts and minds in a way unlikely ever to be undone . . . . We conclude that in the field of public education, the doctrine of 'separate but equal' has no place. Separate educational facilities are inherently unequal."

Thus began the massive upheaval of school desegregation in the United States.

America did not conform gracefully. Twenty bitter years later, communities were still "coming into line" only at the threat of losing federal education funds. Many of the busing plans were obviously costly, ineffective, and downright stupid. Others functioned smoothly. Teachers, parents, and students of all colors and persuasions were frequently inconvenienced. Reverse discrimination suits are now modifying some of the old rules.

In another twenty years, two generations of observers will have a better perspective from which to judge. The feeling here is that, despite many faults, no other decision could have been reached in this land where "all men are created equal."

Right to Abortion: Roe v. Wade *(1973)*

Jane Roe, single and pregnant, wanted an abortion "performed by a competent, licensed physician, under safe, clinical conditions." Her court battle to obtain that abortion, which was forbidden by a Texas statute, brought about one of the most controversial cases in Supreme Court history. Mr. Justice Blackmun wrote the 7–2 decision that gave her that right.

Blackmun noted that most criminal abortion laws were patterned after Victorian legislation where the goal was to discourage illicit sexual conduct, or were enacted because abortions were "hazardous." He concluded that neither situation was valid in 1973, when abortions in the first three months of a pregnancy were as safe as normal childbirth and when the state was no longer concerned with sexual conduct.

The Court found that the Texas statute violated the due process clause of the Fourteenth Amendment as an unjustifiable deprivation of Jane Roe's liberty, infringing upon her right of privacy.

Right of privacy? "Aye, there's the rub," as Hamlet might proclaim. For nowhere in the Constitution of the United States is such a right to be found. "Right to privacy" was drawn by the Warren Court in *Griswold v. Connecticut* (1965)—manufactured, according to detractors, from questionable elements of the Ninth and Fourteenth amendments.

Nevertheless, in the Roe decision, the Court found that the "right of privacy" was broad enough to include a woman's decision to have an abortion. The opinion stated that restrictions on abortions imposed various "detriments" on a pregnant woman, including:

1. Specific and direct harm.
2. "Maternity or additional offspring may force upon the woman a distressful life and future."
3. Psychological harm.
4. Mental and physical health may be taxed.
5. Distress associated with the unwanted child.
6. "The problem of bringing a child into a family already unable . . . to care for it."
7. "Additional difficulties and continued stigma of unwed motherhood."

Blackmun denied that a woman has *unlimited* right to end pregnancy, however. During the first three months of pregnancy, when there is little or no health danger to the mother, the Court ruled that the state may not interfere in a woman's decision. During the last six months, however, when maternal health considerations come into play, the state has a "compelling" interest in the mother's welfare and may regulate abortions to protect maternal health. The Court found that protecting prenatal life was a "legitimate state interest" that was valid during the last ten weeks of pregnancy, when the fetus is *viable* (capable of living outside the womb). During this time, the state may prohibit abortions except where necessary to save the life or health of the mother.

Jane Roe (and millions of "Jane Does") therefore won the right to undergo an abortion under safe, clinical conditions. The finding on the Texas statute affected a host of similar restrictions in a majority of states.

The finding created—and continues to create—an uproar among religious groups and others interested in protecting the life of the unborn. The logic of several statements in the opinion has been violently contested:

"... no case could be cited that a fetus is a person within the meaning of the Fourteenth Amendment."

Nor was there any hint that the word 'person' in the Constitution "... has any possible prenatal application."

"[This study] persuades us that the word 'person' as used in the Fourteenth Amendment, does not include the unborn."

But the most volatile phrase turned out to be "right to privacy."

It was this judicial creation that prompted Mr. Justice Byron White to write, in his minority opinion: "As an exercise of raw judicial power, the Court perhaps has authority to do what it does today; but in my view its judgment is an improvident and extravagant exercise of the power of judicial review ..."

Roe v. Wade promises to stir continuing controversy. We recommend students read "the real thing"—the case itself. Ask any law librarian for *Roe v. Wade*, 410 U.S. 113.

Missouri banned use of its facilities for abortions, forbade its employees from participating, and required other physicians to take viability tests on the unborn child prior to an abortion. In upholding the statute (*Missouri v. Reproductive Health Services (1969)*, the Court appeared to move a step closer to overturning *Roe v. Wade*.

FIRST AMENDMENT RIGHTS

"Clear and Present Danger": Schenck v. U.S. *(1919)*

Schenck, who was secretary of the Socialist Party, and accomplices were convicted of conspiring to cause insubordination in the armed forces and of obstructing recruitment. During World War I they printed fifteen thousand anti-Selective Service leaflets, many mailed to draftees.

Schenck claimed his actions were protected by the First Amendment.

This case is famous for the "clear and present danger" doctrine adopted by the Court and enunciated by Chief Justice Oliver Wendell Holmes. Holmes concluded that if the leaflets constituted a clear and present danger of bringing about evils, Congress had the authority to prevent distribution.

In such an instance, he ruled, "First Amendment freedoms must give way." [In time of war] "many things that might be said in time of peace . . . will not be endured."

School Prayer: Engel v. Vitale *(1962)*

"Almighty God, we acknowledge our dependence upon Thee, and we beg Thy blessings upon us, our parents, our teachers, and our country."

That prayer, recited each morning by children in New York public school classrooms in the early 1960s, sparked a controversy that continues to have tempers flaring in the 1980s. The prayer had been recommended by the New York State Board of Regents and the local school board in New Hyde Park, New York. The parents of ten children challenged the propriety of reciting the prayer in a public classroom, and their case made Supreme Court history.

The Court voted 6 to 1 in favor of the plaintiffs, declaring that the separation of church and state, as expressed in the First Amendment and applied to the states in the Fourteenth Amendment, had clearly been violated. Furthermore, the Court stated that the violation occurred although the prayer was denominationally neutral and children were not forced to recite it. In the Court's view, government-sponsored religious activities were likely to lead to persecution of those who chose not to conform.

RIGHTS OF THE ACCUSED

The Exclusionary Rule: Weeks v. U.S. *(1914)*

Liberals hailed and law enforcement officials wailed in 1914 as the Supreme Court, in *Weeks v. U.S.* established the "exclusionary rule."

"This will allow thousands of guilty people to walk the streets," complained police.

"A small price to pay for our Fourth Amendment freedoms against illegal search and seizure," contended the liberals. "The alternative is a police state."

The "exclusionary rule" said that evidence obtained by illegal search or seizure could not be used in federal courts—even if the violation was technical and police had obtained the warrant in good faith, and *even if the defendant was obviously guilty.*

Although no warrant was issued, Weeks was placed under arrest. His home was searched and papers were taken that were later used to obtain his conviction. He charged his Fourth Amendment rights had been violated.

The Court, in finding for Weeks, took a judicial slap at officers who obtain convictions "by means of illegal seizures and enforced confessions . . . ." It then went on to say: "If letters and private documents can thus be seized and held and used in evidence . . . , the protection of the Fourth Amendment might as well be stricken from the Constitution."

In 1961 the exclusionary rule was applied to the states (*Mapp v. Ohio*).

The Burger Court modified the sting of the exclusionary rule in several decisions:

In *U.S. v. Calandra* (1974), the rule was declared not in effect in grand jury hearings.

In *Stone v. Powell* and *Wolff v. Rice* (1976), the Court ruled that *habeas corpus* relief (releasing defendants) was unnecessary in federal courts where improperly obtained evidence was used.

When defendants in *Rakas v. Illinois* (1978) complained that a gun used in evidence against them was illegally seized from a car, they received no sympathy from the Court, which pointed out that since they claimed they owned neither the gun nor the car they had no constitutional complaint.*

The Court has long recognized that the exclusionary rule is not constitutionally based. Rather, it is a judicially-created rule designed to deter improper police procedure. Many insist it is an ineffective restraint—that it merely results in the nonconviction or nonprosecution of criminals. The Reagan administration, for example, has favored greater reliance upon direct sanctions against improper police conduct rather than the indirect persuasion of the exclusionary rule.

The Supreme Court in *U.S. v. Leon* (1984) created a "good faith" exception to the exclusionary rule. Despite this slight modification, many guilty persons are allowed to walk free from courthouses all over the nation.

The following case illustrates the controversial nature of the exclusionary rule:

On December 26, 1984, an Arizona mother was awakened by the screams of her six-year-old daughter. Racing into the bedroom, she found that the girl had been molested by a prowler.

It had rained that night, and detectives found large muddy footprints inside and outside the home. From the girl's description, detectives checked out a suspect and asked him to come to the station. Reluctantly, he agreed, then went to the bedroom to put on some clothes. Fearful he might emerge with a gun, the two detectives followed him into the house against his objections. One of them picked up a pair of muddy tennis shoes sitting on the oven. The following day the detectives secured a search warrant for the clothes the girl had described and the shoes. The clothes, the footprints, and the man's description all fitted. So did the suspect's record of six sexual convictions. He was tried, convicted, and sentenced to life imprisonment.

The Arizona Supreme Court overturned the conviction. It found the defendant's right of privacy had been invaded because the shoes were picked up

---

* An excellent discussion of these and other modifying cases may be found in *The Supreme Court and Individual Rights* (Washington, D.C.: Congressional Quarterly, Inc., 1980).

before the search warrant was obtained. The state statute read: "No person should be disturbed in his private offices, or his home invaded, without authority of law."

Arizona Assistant Attorney General Steve Twist probably reflected the views of law enforcement people nationwide when he remarked wryly: "A right broad enough, one supposes, to protect [the suspect's] kitchen but not the victim's bedroom."

Do you agree with Mr. Twist? Does the exclusionary rule *really* deter police? Would it be wiser to penalize police than to release a guilty criminal back to society? How would you feel if a detective rang your doorbell, entered your home without being invited, or confiscated as much as a lipstick or a butcher knife? Weigh the conflicting emotions. This is a subject that should generate lively classroom discussion.

Right to Counsel: Gideon v. Wainwright *(1963)*

In the stack of mail addressed to the Supreme Court on January 8, 1962, was a letter from Prisoner No. 003826, Florida State Prison, Raiford, Florida.

The words, penciled on lined sheets, were in careful schoolboy printing. Enclosed was an affidavit requesting permission to proceed "in the form of a pauper," which would waive some procedures and the fee required of those able to pay.

The letter asked the Court to review an order of the Florida State Supreme Court denying a writ of *habeas corpus* because the prisoner had been denied the services of a lawyer in a state felony case.

Clarence Earl Gideon, at the time, was a frail, white-haired, likeable, nonviolent fifty-one-year-old white man who had been in and out of prisons most of his life for having committed felonies. He had no trade, was addicted to gambling, his marriage was a failure. His formal schooling was limited, but his intelligence was not. At the time he was serving five years for breaking into a Panama City, Florida, pool hall with intention of committing a felony.

The trial record showed that Gideon had requested the services of a lawyer and the request was denied. He had told the judge that "The U.S. Supreme Court says I am entitled to be represented by counsel."

The Supreme Court had said nothing of the kind. Twenty years earlier, in *Betts v. Brady*, the Court ruled that defendants in noncapital cases in state courts are not necessarily entitled to a lawyer. Gideon, forced to defend himself, had made mistakes an attorney would not have made.

The story of how the simple petition moved through channels and eventually to prominent Washington attorney Abe Fortas (later, Associate Supreme Court Justice) and a bright young law student, John Hart Ely (later, Dean of Stanford Law School), is an inspiring episode in American judicial history. *Gideon v. Wainwright* (1963) overturned the *Betts* decision and established for all American citizens the right of counsel in state courts. The Fifth Amendment came alive. The case is a landmark.

Gideon was given a new trial and was represented by counsel. He was found innocent. Anthony Lewis, in *Gideon's Trumpet*, traces the story in easy-to-understand prose. It is must reading.

Miranda Rights: Miranda v. Arizona *(1966)*

Twenty-three-year-old Ernesto Miranda was picked up by police shortly after the kidnaping and raping of a young woman in the Phoenix, Arizona, area in 1963. He was quizzed, admitted his guilt, and later tried and convicted.

The verdict was appealed on grounds that the mentally troubled Miranda had not been informed of his Fifth Amendment rights to remain silent, that anything he might say could be used against him, and that he was entitled to confer with counsel.

In an historic decision, the U.S. Supreme Court overturned the conviction. Liberals hailed the verdict as a triumph for human rights and the common man. But the outrage in law enforcement circles was loud and instantaneous.

The conflict was reflected in the minds of the justices themselves. Chief Justice Earl Warren, writing for the majority, referred to "precious rights" defended. Justice Byron White, dissenting, wrote that *Miranda* "will measurably weaken the ability of the criminal law . . . . It is a deliberate calculus to prevent interrogations, to reduce the incidence of confessions and pleas of guilty and to increase the number of trials."

Justice John Harlan wrote of the "heavy-handed and one-sided action . . . so precipitously taken by the Court."

As the twentieth anniversary of *Miranda* passed into history in June 1986, motion picture and television detectives had etched the Miranda impact in the minds of millions of viewers. Every real-life law enforcement officer has a "Miranda card" and takes pains, on making an arrest, to read the accused his or her rights. Dictionaries may some day be forced to accord the term Miranda lowercase prestige.

Juvenile Rights: In re Gault *(1967)*

Gerald Gault was fifteen years old and on probation for a petty theft when arrested by an Arizona sheriff in connection with making an obscene phone call. He was taken to a juvenile home, questioned, and admitted making the call.

In a juvenile court hearing, Gault was found guilty and ordered to a reform school where he could have been held until he was twenty-one. Arizona law did not allow for appeal of juvenile court decisions. When the boy's parents tried to appeal on grounds that the boy's constitutional rights had been violated, the challenge was dismissed.

When the case reached the United States Supreme Court, Arizona attorneys claimed that a juvenile court hearing is not a criminal matter, therefore certain rights guaranteed in adult crimes are not guaranteed.

The Court found that juveniles, as well as adults, are entitled to basic civil rights. It ruled that Gault had not been informed of his Miranda rights, had been denied right of counsel, right of appeal, and the right to a transcript.

Mr. Justice Fortas, in writing the decision for the Court, commented: "Under our Constitution, the condition of being a boy does not justify a kangaroo court."

Ironically, if Gault had been twenty-one when he committed the offense, he would have been subject to a maximum fine of fifty dollars and imprisonment for a maximum of two months. *In re Gault* wiped out this type of second class citizenship. The American Bar Association, in a 1974 poll, rated this decision as one of eighteen milestone events in American Judicial history.

QUESTIONS

1. The John Marshall quote, "the power to tax is the power to destroy," was written for which case?
2. Name the case in which Robert Fulton, inventor of the steamboat, was involved.
3. Explain the following fictitious citation: *Students v. Professors,* 278 U.S. 372 at 374, 1987.
4. The case of *McCulloch v. Maryland* is famous for the development of what doctrine?
5. The "commerce clause" was interpreted as a congressional power in what case?
6. The case of *Plessy v. Ferguson* established a doctrine that was not overturned for fifty-seven years. What was the doctrine?
7. What were "Jim Crow" laws?
8. Name the Supreme Court justice who wrote a classic dissent on the Court's "separate but equal" decision.
9. Why was this dissent so remarkable?
10. Who was Jane Roe?
11. The right of judicial review was established in which case?
12. What is the doctrine established by Chief Justice Holmes in *Schenck v. U.S.* that said, in effect, that freedom of speech and of the press are not absolute?
13. Who was the attorney for the defense in the case of *Dartmouth College v. Woodward?*
14. In what case was the exclusionary rule established?

15. What is the exclusionary rule?

16. What 1962 case gave increased political power to urban voters?

17. What other voting phenomenon occurred in the second half of the twentieth century?

18. Historically, what has been the general attitude of the Supreme Court on presidential power?

19. What was the most surprising facet of the Court's 8–0 decision against Richard Nixon?

20. What historic occurrence took place two weeks after the decision in *U.S. v. Nixon*?

21. Why did Justice Rehnquist disqualify himself in the *Nixon* case?

22. What case established that the doctrine of separate-but-equal public school facilities is unequal and therefore unconstitutional?

23. What black organization participated in the court battle for equal educational facilities?

24. What was the public reaction to the decision?

25. Who was the Chief Justice who encouraged the Court to act unanimously in this case?

26. Why did the Court say that Dred Scott was not entitled to bring suit in federal court?

27. In the *Dred Scott* case, what Act of 1820 was ruled unconstitutional?

28. Why did the Court rule that Scott's living for five years on free soil did not make him a free man?

29. How and when was the "necessary and proper" clause (Article I, Section 8) applied by John Marshall?

30. What two clauses of what amendment have probably had the most profound impact on human rights decisions of the second half of the twentieth century?

See Answers to Questions, pp. 174–75.

7

The Constitution of the United States

It is time to examine the Constitution itself section by section, sometimes paragraph by paragraph. In this brief introduction we would like to stress two significant points:

1. The concept of *republicanism*, or representative government, which dominates the American Constitution.
2. The importance of understanding the structure and sequence of the document, thus simplifying the process of locating almost any reference in a few seconds.

OUR REPUBLICAN GOVERNMENT

The finest example of *democracy* in America probably was the New England town meeting, where people came in person to listen and debate, to protest and politick and vote.

Our Constitution establishes a *republican* form of government—one administered by representatives elected by the people. These delegates are not under obligation to act according to the wishes of any majority. The American electorate's most powerful weapon is the right to vote out of office any representative who does not properly represent.

It was *representatives* (members of state legislatures) who chose the delegates to the Philadelphia convention.

It was *representatives* chosen in special state elections who voted "aye" or "nay" on ratification.

It would be *representatives* of the people—the president, vice-president and congressmen—who would administer the government.

In many states and municipalities today the people may take direct action through the initiative, referendum, and recall. Our federal government does not include these features.

Nor do we have a voice in naming cabinet members, federal judges, or ambassadors. That job is mandated to a *representative* in the White House, with the "advice and consent" of other *representatives*—members of the Senate.

Even in selecting a president and vice-president, Patrick and Patricia Patriot do not cast direct ballots. They vote, instead, for electors.

James Madison, as we have seen on page 30, defined and stressed the republican concept in *The Federalist Papers*. Serious students of the Constitution should never forget it as they study the document's immortal words.

UNDERSTANDING THE CONSTITUTION

Once you are aware of the *structure* of the Constitution, finding passages is simple. Like almost all complex organizations—libraries, universities, corporations, chests of drawers—this magnificent document is neatly compartmentalized. Your supermarket is divided into *departments* (bakery, meat), subdivided into *divisions* (cakes, pies, bread), and further broken down by *shelves* (whole wheat, rye, white, or by brand names).

Our constitutional supermarket labels its divisions *Articles, Sections,* and *Paragraphs.* Spend a few minutes studying this structure and looking for *frozen foods,* then *ice cream,* then your favorite *brand.*

The key to remembering approximate locations is elementary. *The seven articles fall in logical order according to their importance in the minds of the Founding Fathers.* Students can find almost anything in the Constitution within seconds if they note this order of priority and logical sequence in the seven articles:

It was first necessary to establish the three branches. The Legislative, stemming from the people, was considered the most important and was marked "Article I"; next came the Executive (Article II); and the Judicial (Article III). Nobody dreamed the Judiciary would ever ascend to its lofty twentieth century role.

With the three branches established, it was necessary to give the new nation credibility. Article IV gave "full faith and credit" to public acts, documents, and records of the several states, establishing unity and respectability among equally sovereign states.

Next, it was necessary to contemplate change. Article V, the amending article, handled that challenge.

At this point, just as in the establishment of any late twentieth century corporation, it was vital to establish a reputation for honesty and integrity. Article VI promised a watchful outside world that the United States, under new man-

DID THE FOUNDING FATHERS GOOF?

While finding clauses in the original Constitution is easy, the study of changes caused by amendments becomes a bit complex. This is because the founders left to posterity the problem of incorporating amendments into the original text.

Error number one was in calling the amendments *articles*. Result: non-scholars for two hundred years have, for instance, occasionally confused Article III (Judiciary) with Article 3 (the Third Amendment). This book will call amendments *amendments*.

But the problem is not limited to terminology. When a reader finds a clause affected by an amendment, he must find that amendment, then compare it with the original wording.

James Madison clearly foresaw such a problem. He suggested to the first Congress that amendments be incorporated into the original text at the point where they become relevant. But the Senate turned down the suggestion.

To illustrate: On presidential terms, Article II, Section 1 reads, "He shall hold office during the term of four years."

A student doing his homework in Rome or Vienna or an alien cramming for his citizenship exam in Cleveland could be excused for thinking a president is limited to one term or that there are no restrictions. It's easy to miss the Twenty-second Amendment, many pages away.

How much simpler to handle it Madison's way: "He shall hold his office during the term of four years. . . . No person shall be elected to the office . . . more than twice. . . . "

Under Madison's plan the thirsty soul who reads ". . . the manufacture, sale, or transportation of intoxicating liquors is hereby prohibited" in the Eighteenth Amendment would be immediately calmed to see in the Twenty-first Amendment that "The eighteenth Article of amendment . . . is hereby repealed."

It's a plan that would win the enthusiastic approval of every history teacher in the United States.

---

agement, would assume responsibility for all debts and promises contracted by the old Confederation. It also underscored the sanctity of "This Constitution . . . the laws of the United States . . . and all treaties" as "the supreme law of the land . . . ."

Article VII provided for the method of ratification.

Students are again reminded to note the descending order of importance of the seven articles, beginning with the most important, Article I, the Legislative. Paragraph 1 of Article VI was unnecessary as soon as the last invoice of the old government was stamped "paid." Article VII accomplished its mission upon ratification.

The sections within the articles also usually follow in order of importance. The exceptions are for the purpose of clarity and logical sequence. Thus, Section 1 of Article I establishes a Congress; Section 2 deals with the most important branch, the House of Representatives; Section 3 deals with the Senate; and Sections 4 through 10 return to the bicameral Congress to deal with elections, rules, compensation, the process of legislation, the veto, enumerated powers, restrictions, etc.

THE CONSTITUTION

Preamble

We, the people of the United States, in order to form a more perfect Union, establish justice, insure domestic tranquility, provide for the common defence, promote the general welfare, and secure the blessings of liberty to ourselves and our posterity, do ordain and establish this Constitution for the United States of America.

The Preamble is one of the best known and most expertly crafted sentences in world constitutional history. The first words establish the source of sovereignty. The next forty-five capture the essence of almost four months of philosophical debate. The preamble is a statement of purpose, a reason for being, a rationale for presenting the script by which Americans would consent to be governed.

Primarily the work of Gouvernor Morris, the preamble is a literary as well as a political triumph. The verbs are crisp, dynamic, and alive; the goals summarize universal dreams; and the almost metrical cadence is most noticeable when the lines are set in verse form and recited aloud.

Article I—The Legislative

Section 1

Legislative Powers Vested in Congress. All legislative powers herein granted shall be vested in a Congress of the United States, which shall consist of a Senate and House of Representatives.

Gray shaded areas represent the author's explanations and comments.

Section 2

Section 2 deals exclusively with the House of Representatives.

Composition of the House of Representatives. 1. The House of Representatives shall be composed of members chosen every second year by the people of the several States, and the electors in each State shall have the qualifications requisite for electors of the most numerous branch of the State Legislature.

The *states* set qualifications for electors (voters) in federal elections. Certain acts of Congress and certain amendments (the Fifteenth, Nineteenth, Twenty-fourth, and Twenty-sixth) have since abridged state authority.

Qualifications of Representatives. 2. No Person shall be a Representative who shall not have attained the age of twenty-five years, and been seven years a citizen of the United States, and who shall not, when elected, be an inhabitant of that State in which he shall be chosen.

Note the term "inhabitant" instead of "legal resident," and that senators also may be merely "inhabitants" (Section 3, paragraph 3). Such a distinction enabled Robert Kennedy to be elected senator from New York in 1964. An "inhabitant" of New York but still a "registered voter" and probably a legal resident of Massachusetts, Kennedy had not lived in New York long enough to meet the state's voting requirements. College students and members of the armed forces are often confronted with the problem of "legal residency" status.

Apportionment of Representatives and Census. 3. [Representatives and direct taxes shall be apportioned among the several States which may be included within this Union, according to their respective numbers, which shall be determined by adding to the whole number of free persons, including those bound to service for a term of years and excluding Indians not taxed, three fifths of all other persons.] The actual enumeration shall be made within three years after the first meeting of the Congress of the United States, and within every subsequent term of ten years, in such manner as they shall by law direct. The number of Representatives shall not exceed one for every thirty thousand, but each State shall have at least one Representative; and until such enumeration shall be made, the State of New Hampshire shall be entitled to choose three, Massachusetts eight, Rhode Island and Providence Plantations one,

---

Subject headings, which do not appear in the original document, are modifications of those to be found in *State of New Hamphire Manual for the General Court* (Concord, N.H., 1969), pp. 15–42. •

Connecticut five, New York six, New Jersey four, Pennsylvania eight, Delaware one, Maryland six, Virginia ten, North Carolina five, South Carolina five, and Georgia three.

> The bracketed first sentence was rendered obsolete by passage of the Fourteenth Amendment, ratified in 1868.
> "Other persons" is a fancy term for slaves.

Vacancies.   4. When vacancies happen in the representation from any State, the Executive Authority thereof shall issue writs of election to fill such vacancies.

> "The Executive Authority thereof" is the governor.

Selection of Officers; Impeachment.   5. The House of Representatives shall choose their Speaker and other officers; and shall have the sole power of impeachment.

Section 3

> Section 3 deals exclusively with the Senate.

The Senate.   [1. The Senate of the United States shall be composed of two Senators from each State, chosen by the Legislature thereof, for six years; and each Senator shall have one vote.]

> Senators are now elected directly by the people, a change brought about by the Seventeenth Amendment, ratified in 1913.

Classification of Senators; Vacancies.   2. Immediately after they shall be assembled in consequence of the first election, they shall be divided as equally as may be into three classes. The seats of the Senators of the first class shall be vacated at the expiration of the second year, of the second class at the expiration of the fourth year, and of the third class at the expiration of the sixth year, so that one third may be chosen every second year; and if vacancies happen by resignation, or otherwise, during the recess of the Legislature of any State, the Executive thereof may make temporary appointments [until the next meeting of the Legislature, which shall then fill such vacancies.]

> "And if vacancies happen . . . appointments"—this was the entranceway that first brought a woman into the Senate. When Senator Thaddeus Caraway died in 1931, Arkansas Governor Harvey Parnell

temporarily appointed Caraway's widow to succeed her husband. In 1932 Hattie Caraway won a special election for the unexpired term, then was reelected to two six-year terms. The bracketed sentence was canceled by the Seventeenth Amendment.

Qualification of Senators. 3. No person shall be a Senator who shall not have attained to the age of thirty years, and been nine years a citizen of the United States, and who shall not, when elected, be an inhabitant of that State for which he shall be chosen.

The founders believed that the Senate required a more mature person than the House. Hence, the thirty years of age and nine years a citizen requirement. (Compare with twenty-five and seven for a Representative.) Note again the word "inhabitant" instead of "legal resident" or "registered voter."

Vice President. 4. The Vice President of the United States shall be President of the Senate, but shall have no vote, unless they be equally divided.

George Mifflin Dallas, vice-president under President James Polk, displayed sterling integrity by casting his tie-breaking vote in favor of a tariff bill that both Dallas and his home state of Pennsylvania violently opposed. But Dallas believed it was his duty to support the president. Dallas was hanged in effigy, denounced by the Pennsylvania press, and never returned to favor. One out-of-state headline read: NO MORE VICE PRESIDENTS FROM PENNSYLVANIA. Through 1987, he remains the state's only vice-president.

Senate Officers; President pro Tempore. 5. The Senate, shall choose their other officers, and also a President pro tempore, in the absence of the Vice President, or when he shall exercise the office of President of the United States.

Senate to Try Impeachment. 6. The Senate shall have the sole power to try all impeachments. When sitting for that purpose, they shall be on oath or affirmation. When the President of the United States is tried, the Chief Justice shall preside: And no person shall be convicted without the concurrence of two thirds of the members present.

Note that the House impeaches and the Senate conducts the trial. Sitting as jurors, senators take an oath similar to that taken by jurors in standard courts. Their authority is much the same as that of any court. They may force a witness to appear and may demand answers, under threat of a contempt citation.

Andrew Johnson, the only president to be impeached, was found not guilty by the courageous vote of Senator Edmund G. Ross of Kansas. A memorable account of Ross's political suicide is found in John Kennedy's *Profiles in Courage* in the chapter entitled, "I . . . Looked Down into My Open Grave."

Judgment in Case of Impeachment.   7. Judgment in cases of impeachment shall not extend further than to removal from office, and disqualification to hold and enjoy any office of honor, trust, or profit under the United States: but the party convicted shall nevertheless be liable and subject to indictment, trial, judgment and punishment, according to law.

Fourteen men have been impeached and five convicted in the first 200 years under the Constitution. The 14 include one president, one senator, one secretary of war, and 11 federal judges, one of whom was a member of the Supreme Court. The five found guilty were lower court judges. In 1974 the House Judiciary Committee recommended impeachment of President Nixon on three counts. Facing almost certain impeachment and probable conviction, he resigned in August of that year.

Section 4

Control of Congressional Elections.   1. The times, places and manner of holding elections for Senators and Representatives, shall be prescribed in each State by the Legislature thereof; but the Congress may at any time by law make or alter such regulations, except as to the places of choosing Senators.

In 1845 Congress established election day as the Tuesday after the first Monday in November. Why this date? The date fell approximately one month before electors were required to gather to cast their votes for president and vice president; Tuesday was chosen instead of Monday so that people who were forced to travel a long distance would not have to start on Sunday, a day of worship. The Tuesday after the first Monday was selected to guard against an election day falling on the first of the month—a courtesy to business interests. Why did Congress establish a national election day? With different election days in different states, it was not uncommon for politicians to transport wagonloads of men across state lines to cast ballots in key districts. Also, news of the vote in one state tended to influence the balloting in other states. In today's electronic age, "exit poll" results in New York can affect voting in western states.

For the first fifty-three years of the Constitution, a voter cast ballots for as many representatives as his state was assigned. Under such a system, many sparsely populated areas were denied any representation. In 1842 Congress ordered that states be divided into Congressional Districts and that the people from each District elect one man as their representative in the House.

Time for Assembling of Congress. 2. The Congress shall assemble at least once in every year, and such meeting shall be on the first Monday in December, unless they shall by law appoint a different day.

Here, the Founding Fathers carefully guarded against an abuse practiced by English kings, who often tried to rule without Parliament. Charles I's eleven years of "personal rule" (1629–40) brought him to the brink of the Civil War which cost him his head. Charles' father, James I, ruled for ten years during which only one Parliament—the "Addled Parliament"—met for only a few days and was dismissed by the king. The time of assembling was changed by the Twentieth Amendment.

Section 5

Election and Qualifications of Members; Quorum. 1. Each House shall be the judge of the elections, returns and qualifications of its own members, and a majority of each shall constitute a quorum to do business; but a smaller number may adjourn from day to day, and may be authorized to compel the attendance of absent members, in such manner, and under such penalties as each House may provide.

A quorum is more than half of the members. Constitutional scholars are not at all certain that a member of Congress may be impeached. Senator Blount was impeached in 1798 but resigned before the case came to trial in the Senate. This is the only impeachment in Congressional history and the ruling at that time—that the Senate did not have jurisdiction—has never again been tested.

Two notable instances in which the Congress punished its own members occurred in recent times: In December 1954, the Senate formally condemned Senator Joseph McCarthy (Rep., Wis.) for conduct "contrary to Senate traditions." In 1967 the House excluded Adam Clayton Powell (Dem., N.Y.), alleging he had made improper expenditures of public funds for private purposes. In a special election the following year, Powell's Harlem constituents overwhelmingly returned him to office. Although seated, he was deprived of his senority and fined $25,000. In June 1969, the Supreme Court ruled that the House had unconstitutionally excluded Powell.

Each House to Determine Its Own Rules. 2. Each House may determine the rules of its proceedings, punish its members for disorderly behavior, and, with the concurrence of two thirds, expel a member.

Journals and Yeas and Nays. 3. Each House shall keep a journal of its proceedings, and from time to time publish the same, *excepting such parts as may in their judgment require secrecy;* and the yeas and nays of the members of either House on any question shall, at the desire of one fifth of those present, be entered on the journal.

Delicate matters such as treaties and discussions concerning personalities and appointments may be discussed secretly. This often comes as a surprise to the general public.

Adjournment. 4. Neither House, during the session of Congress, shall, without the consent of the other, adjourn for more than three days, nor to any other place than that in which the two Houses shall be sitting.

Section 6

Compensation and Privileges of Members of Congress. 1. The Senators and Representatives shall receive a compensation for their services, to be ascertained by law, and paid out of the Treasury of the United States. They shall in all cases, except treason, felony and breach of the peace, be privileged from arrest during their attendance at the session of their respective Houses, and in going to and returning from the same; and for any speech or debate in either House, they shall not be questioned in any other place.

Salaries as of January, 1991: Representatives, $125,100; Senators (lower because Senate voted to keep certain honorariums), $101,400.

Incompatible Offices. 2. No Senator or Representative shall, during the time for which he was elected, be appointed to any civil office under the authority of the United States, which shall have been created, or the emoluments whereof shall have been increased during such time; and no person holding any office under the United States, shall be a member of either House during his continuance in office.

No federal moonlighting.

Section 7

Revenue Bills.   1. All bills for raising revenue shall originate in the House of Representatives; but the Senate may propose or concur with amendments as on other bills.

An extremely foresighted stipulation. The Senate is composed of two members from each state, regardless of size. Though states with large populations would bear a disproportionate amount of the expense of some revenue bills, small and medium-size states could outvote them in the Senate if that body were allowed to introduce revenue measures. Comparable, in a large family, to allowing the children to vote on all budget matters.

Manner of Passing Bills; Veto Power of President.   2. Every bill which shall have passed the House of Representatives and the Senate, shall before it becomes a law, be presented to the President of the United States; If he approves he shall sign it, but if not he shall return it, with his objections to the House in which it shall have originated, who shall enter the objections at large on their journal, and proceed to reconsider it. If after such reconsideration two thirds of that House shall agree to pass the bill, it shall be sent, together with the objections, to the other House, by which it shall likewise be reconsidered, and if approved by two thirds of that House, it shall become a law. But in all such Cases the Votes of both Houses shall be determined by yeas and nays, and the names of the persons voting for and against the bill shall be entered on the journal of each House respectively. If any bill shall not be returned by the President within ten days (Sundays excepted) after it shall have been presented to him, the same shall be a law, in like manner as if he had signed it, unless the Congress by their adjournment prevent its return, in which case it shall not be a Law.

The requirement that every bill passed by Congress must be presented to the president for his signature is important. Since the president takes much of the credit or blame, this requirement insures (at least theoretically) that no legislation may be slipped by him.

The word "veto" means, literally, "I forbid."

Consider what a powerful tool the presidential veto is! If the president says "I forbid," both houses must pass the bill by a two-thirds vote.

There are no more oral "yeas" and "nays." The Reorganization Act of 1970 approved voting by electronic method in the House and the system was installed and placed in operation with the beginning of the 93rd Congress in January 1973.

This withholding is known as a "pocket veto." The pocket veto is often employed by presidents when a great number of bills are rushed to them in the closing days of the session. Rather than write long and hasty objections, presidents "put the bills in their pockets" and thus prevent passage.

(Some state constitutions have provisions by which the governor may veto parts of a bill. The U.S. Constitution has no such provision: a veto of any part constitutes a veto of the whole. The controversial "Boland Amendment" was attached to a critical appropriations bill. President Reagan could not veto the Boland measure without killing the much-needed revenue measure. Statistics dramatically prove the power of the veto: through the adjournment of the 92nd Congress in 1972, Congress overrode the presidential veto only seventy-seven times. Andrew Johnson was overridden most often—fifteen times; Presidents Tyler, Hayes, Arthur, Benjamin Harrison, Theodore Roosevelt, and Taft each suffered only a single override; Richard Nixon's last full session (the 92nd) found him overturned only twice.) Four men, Cleveland with 584 vetoes (and seven overrides), Truman, 250 (twelve), Eisenhower, 181 (two), and Franklin Roosevelt, 631 (nine), accounted for 1,646 of the approximately 2,300 vetoes in American History through the Nixon resignation (through January 1, 1976, Ford vetoed forty-two measures and suffered six overrides). Of 3,079 measures sent to President Carter, thirty-one were vetoed and two were overridden. Ronald Reagan, in his first term of office, was presented with 1,135 bills, He vetoed thirty-nine; only four were overridden. Most of Cleveland's vetoes concerned small, private pensions. At the other extreme, Adams and Jefferson did not exercise the veto power once in their twelve years.

Concurrent Orders or Resolutions.   3. Every order, resolution, or vote to which the concurrence of the Senate and House of Representatives may be necessary (except on a question of adjournment) shall be presented to the President of the United States; and before the same shall take effect, shall be approved by him, or being disapproved by him, shall be repassed by two thirds of the Senate and House of Representatives, according to the rule and limitations prescribed in the case of a bill.

Section 8   The Congress Shall Have Power

These are the so-called "enumerated" powers of the Congress.

Taxes.   1. To lay and collect taxes, duties, imposts and excises, to pay the debts and provide for the common defence and general welfare of the United States; but all duties, imposts and excises shall be uniform throughout the United States.

Borrowing.   2. To borrow money on the credit of the United States.

A common method is war bonds, called "Liberty Bonds" during World War I.

Regulation of Commerce.   3. To regulate commerce with foreign nations, and among the several States, and with the Indian tribes.

This is the powerful "commerce clause" which Congress and the courts have currently interpreted as giving the Congress almost unlimited power to regulate business. It is difficult to conceive of a business transaction, no matter how local in concept, that cannot be interpreted as coming under "interstate commerce."

Naturalization and Bankruptcy.   4. To establish a uniform rule of naturalization, and uniform laws on the subject of bankruptcies throughout the United States.

Money, Weights and Measures.   5. To coin money, regulate the value thereof, and of foreign coin, and fix the standard of weights and measures.

Counterfeiting.   6. To provide for the punishment of counterfeiting the securities and current coin of the United States.

Post Offices.   7. To establish post offices and post roads.

Patents and Copyrights.   8. To promote the progress of science and useful arts, by securing for limited times to authors and inventors the exclusive right to their respective writings and discoveries.

Inferior Courts.   9. To constitute tribunals inferior to the Supreme Court.

Piracies and Felonies.   10. To define and punish piracies and felonies committed on the high seas, and offenses against the law of nations.

War.   11. To declare war, grant letters of marque and reprisal, make rules concerning captures on land and water.

> Written authorizations allowing a citizen to seize persons or property of another state, or to fit out and arm a ship for the purpose of attacking enemy ships.

Armies.   12. To raise and support armies, but no appropriation of money to that use shall be for a longer term than two years.

Navy.   13. To provide and maintain a navy.

Land and Naval Forces.   14. To make rules for the government and regulation of the land and naval forces.

Calling Out Militia.   15. To provide for calling forth the militia to execute the laws of the Union, suppress insurrections and repel invasions.

Organizing, Arming and Disciplining Militia.   16. To provide for organizing, arming, and disciplining the militia, and for governing such part of them as may be employed in the service of the United States, reserving to the States, respectively, the appointment of the officers, and the authority of training the militia according to the discipline prescribed by Congress.

District of Columbia.   17. To exercise exclusive legislation in all cases whatsoever, over such district (not exceeding ten miles square) as may, by cession of particular states, and the acceptance of Congress, become the seat of the Government of the United States, and to exercise like authority over all places purchased by the consent of the Legislature of the State in which the same shall be, for the erection of forts, magazines, arsenals, dockyards, and other needful buildings;—And

To Enact Laws Necessary to Enforce Constitution.   18. To make all laws which shall be necessary and proper for carrying into execution the foregoing powers, and all other powers vested by this Constitution in the Government of the United States, or in any department or office thereof.

> This is the famous "necessary and proper" or "implied powers" clause, the fountain from which many of the *assumed* powers of Congress flows. Its current interpretation is vigorously protested by states' righters. See *McCulloch v. Maryland*, p. 98.

Section 9

> This section contains prohibitions on the Congress.

Slave Trade.   1. The migration or importation of such persons as any of the States now existing shall think proper to admit, shall not be prohibited by the Congress prior to the year one thousand eight hundred and eight, but a tax or duty may be imposed on such importation, not exceeding ten dollars for each person.

Writ of Habeas Corpus.   2. The privilege of the writ of habeas corpus shall not be suspended, unless when in cases of rebellion or invasion the public safety may require it.

Bills of Attainder and Ex Post Facto Laws Prohibited.   3. No bill of attainder or *ex post facto* law shall be passed.

> A bill of attainder "attaints" the family of a criminal, usually by a denial of civil rights. Once common in England.
>   *Ex post facto* means "after the fact." Applying a new law to an action committed *before passage*.

Capitation and Other Direct Taxes.   4. No capitation, or other direct tax shall be laid, unless in proportion to the census or enumeration herein before directed to be taken.

> "By head." For example, an arbitrary tax of twenty-five dollars per person per year, regardless of income or other considerations.

Exports Not to Be Taxed.   5. No tax or duty shall be laid on articles exported from any State.

Shipping.   6. No preference shall be given by any regulation of commerce or revenue to the ports of one State over those of another; nor shall vessels bound to, or from, one State, be obliged to enter, clear, or pay duties in another.

Appropriations; Reports.   7. No money shall be drawn from the Treasury, but in consequence of appropriations made by law; and a regular statement and account of the receipts and expenditures of all public money shall be published from time to time.

Titles of Nobility; Favors from Foreign Powers.   8. No title of nobility shall be granted by the United States: And no person holding any office of profit or trust under them, shall without the consent of the Congress, accept of any present, emolument, office, or title, of any kind whatever, from any king, prince, or foreign state.

Section 10

> This section contains prohibitions on the states. Students should be particularly careful not to confuse the prohibitions on the Congress

(Section 9) with the prohibitions of the States (Section 10). *This is one of the foremost traps in constitutional examinations!*

Limitations of the Powers of the Several States. 1. No State shall enter into any treaty, alliance, or confederation; grant letters of marque and reprisal; coin money; emit bills of credit; make anything but gold and silver coin a tender in payment of debts; pass any bill of attainder, ex post facto law, or law impairing the obligation of contracts or grant any title of nobility.

State Imposts and Duties. 2. No State shall, without the consent of the Congress, lay any imposts or duties on imports or exports, except what may be absolutely necessary for executing its inspection laws; and the net produce of all duties and imports, laid by any State on imports or exports, shall be for the use of the Treasury of the United States; and all such laws shall be subject to the revision and control of the Congress.

Further Restrictions on Powers of States. 3. No State shall, without the consent of Congress, lay any duty of tonnage, keep troops, or ships of war in time of peace, enter into any agreement or compact with another State, or with a foreign power, or engage in war, unless actually invaded, or in such imminent danger as will not admit of delay.

The enumerated powers presented in Section 8 are models of clarity that have stood the test of time. In a few hundred words, they spell out work instructions of the Congress. When balanced with the restrictions on Congress that appear in Section 9 and restrictions on the states outlined in Section 10, (and tempered by a test of constitutionality as interpreted by the Supreme Court) these powers constitute a remarkable blueprint for running a government.

It is probable that if the Founding Fathers had a crystal ball they would have included a precise definition of the word "commerce" in Paragraph 3 of Section 8. But the "necessary and proper" clause (Paragraph 18), though sometimes abused and often maligned, has proved to be an indispensable (and necessary and proper) congressional tool. The founders conceived it as the instrument for handling most of the problems they could not anticipate. Generally, Paragraph 18 has served its purpose.

Article II—The Executive

Section 1

The President; the Executive Power. 1. The Executive power shall be vested in a President of the United States of America. He shall hold his office during the term of four years, and, together with the Vice President, chosen for the same term, be elected, as follows:

The Constitutional Convention considered an executive department of two or more individuals, but decided that more decisive action would result if responsibility were vested in one person. The question of whether a president could run for reelection was debated but not acted upon. George Washington set a 144-year precedent by running for re-election and firmly declining a third term. The Twenty-second Amendment (1951) limited the presidency to two full terms.

Appointment and Qualifications of Presidential Electors. 2. Each State shall appoint, in such manner as the legislature thereof may direct, a number of electors, equal to the whole number of Senators and Representatives to which the State may be entitled in the Congress; but no Senator or Representative or person holding an office of trust or profit under the United States, shall be appointed an elector.

The word "electors" here refers to electoral college members. However, the same work in Article I means an authorized voter.

This paragraph is obsolete. It was replaced by the Twelfth Amendment, which was prompted by the political fiasco in which Aaron Burr almost stole the presidency from Thomas Jefferson in 1800. See comment on the Twelfth Amendment, p. 57.

Original Method of Electing the President and Vice-President. [The electors shall meet in their respective States, and vote by ballot for two persons, of whom one at least shall not be an inhabitant of the same state with themselves. And they shall make a list of all the persons voted for, and of the number of votes for each; which list they shall sign and certify, and transmit sealed to the seat of the Government of the United States, directed to the President of the Senate. The President of the Senate shall, in the presence of the Senate and House of Representatives, open all the certificates, and the votes shall then be counted. The person having the greatest number of votes shall be the President, if such number be a majority of the whole number of electors appointed; and if there be more than one who have such majority, and have an equal number of votes, then the House of Representatives shall immediately choose by ballot one of them for President; and if no person have a majority, then from the five highest on the list the said House shall in like manner choose the President. But in choosing the President, the votes shall be taken by States, the representation from each State having one vote; a quorum for this purpose shall consist of a member or members from two thirds of the States, and a majority of all the States shall be necessary to a choice. In every case, after the choice of the President, the person having the greatest number of votes of the electors shall be the Vice President. But if there should remain two or more who have equal votes, the Senate shall choose from them by ballot the Vice President.]

Electors. 3. The Congress may determine the time of choosing the electors, and the day on which they shall give their votes; which day shall be the same throughout the United States.

First Tuesday after the first Monday in November. Electors officially cast their votes on the Monday following the second Wednesday in December.

Qualifications for President. 4. No person except a natural born citizen, *or a citizen of the United States, at the time of the adoption of this Constitution,* shall be eligible to the office of President; neither shall any person be eligible to that office who shall not have attained to the age of thirty-five years, and been fourteen years a resident within the United States.

No naturalized citizen has ever become president, and for more than a century the Constitution has forbidden such an eventuality. But note carefully the clause in italics. The clause *could have* permitted West Indian-born Alexander Hamilton or Swiss-born Albert Gallatin, Jefferson's secretary of the treasury, or other foreign-born citizens of that day to be elected president.

Filling Vacancy in the Office of President. 5. In case of the removal of the President from office, or of his death, resignation, or inability to discharge the powers and duties of the said office, the same shall devolve on the Vice President, and the Congress may by law provide for the case of removal, death, resignation or inability, both of the President and Vice President, declaring what officer shall then act as President, and such officer shall act accordingly, until the disability be removed, or a President shall be elected.

A highly controversial clause. The question of what constitutes "inability to discharge the powers and duties" is not defined. The clause caused concern during periods of disability suffered by Woodrow Wilson, Dwight Eisenhower, and Lyndon B. Johnson. The replacement of Vice-President Spiro Agnew and, later, of President Richard Nixon was covered by the Twenty-fifth Amendment of 1967.

When Vice-President John Tyler succeeded President William Henry Harrison in 1841, he immediately assumed that the Constitution clothed him with all the authority (and salary and perquisites) of the office. The precedent he established has never again been questioned.

Paragraph 5 also authorizes Congress to name the order of succession when both the president and vice president have vacated their offices. The Presidential Succession Law of 1947, since amended four times, covers this contingency.

Compensation of the President. 6. The President shall, at stated times, receive for his services, a compensation, which shall neither be increased nor diminished during the period for which he shall have been elected, and he shall not receive within that period any other emolument from the United States, or any of them.

Through 1988 the president's salary is $200,000; the vice-president receives $115,000, but his salary is subject to adjustment. The presidential salary remains the same while a president is in office, because the Founding Fathers feared Congress might use its wage-setting powers to punish, bribe, or reward.

Oath to Be Taken by the President. 7. Before he enter on the execution of his office, he shall take the following oath or affirmation:—"I do solemnly swear (or affirm) that I will faithfully execute the office of President of the United States, and will to the best of my ability, preserve, protect and defend the Constitution of the United States."

Section 2

The President to Be Commander-in-Chief and Head of Executive Department; Reprieves and Pardons. 1. The President shall be Commander-in-Chief of the Army and Navy of the United States, and of the militia of the several States, when called into the actual service of the United States; he may require the opinion, in writing, of the principal officer in each of the executive departments, upon any subject relating to the duties of their respective offices, and he shall have power to grant reprieves and pardons for offenses against the United States, except in cases of impeachment.

Treaties; Ambassadors; Inferior Officers. 2. He shall have power, by and with the advice and consent of the Senate to make treaties, provided two thirds of the Senators present concur; and he shall nominate, and by and with the advice and consent of the Senate, shall appoint ambassadors, other public ministers and consuls, judges of the Supreme Court, and all other officers of the United States, whose appointments are not herein otherwise provided for, and which shall be established by law; but the Congress may by law vest the appointment of such inferior officers, as they think proper, in the President alone, in the courts of law, or in the heads of departments.

President May Fill Vacancies in Office during Recess of Senate. 3. The President shall have the power to fill all vacancies that may happen during the recess of the Senate, by granting commissions, which shall expire at the end of their next session.

All three paragraphs of Section 2 deal with the powers of the president. Note that the reprieve and pardon powers extend only to offenses in *federal* cases.

Section 3

President to Give Advice to Congress; May Convene or Adjourn It on Certain Occasions; to Receive Ambassadors, etc.; Have Laws Executed and Commission All Officers. He shall from time to time give to the Congress information of the state of the Union, and recommend to their consideration such measures as he shall judge necessary and expedient; he may, on extraordinary occasions, convene both Houses, or either of them, and in case of disagreement between them, with respect to the time of adjournment, he may adjourn them to such time as he shall think proper; he shall receive ambassadors and other public ministers; he shall take care that the laws be faithfully executed, and shall commission all the officers of the United States.

Section 3 spells out the required duties of the president.

The president has the option of delivering the state of the union address before a joint session of the Congress, or of sending the message to be read. Most modern presidents have delivered the address in person, in the full glare of coverage by all the major television and radio networks. The state of the union message is one of the first orders of business in every new Congress; another important speech is the budget message.

No president has ever adjourned Congress.

Section 4

All Civil Officers Removable by Impeachment. The President, Vice President, and all civil officers of the United States, shall be removed from office on impeachment for, and conviction of, treason, bribery, or other high crimes and misdemeanors.

The definition of "other high crimes and misdemeanors" has never been satisfactorily settled. Only the Senate, sitting as a court of impeachment, can make this determination. There is no appeal from an impeachment conviction, not even to the Supreme Court.

Article III—The Judiciary

Section 1

Judicial Power; Term of Office and Compensation of Judges.   The judicial power of the United States shall be vested in one Supreme Court, and in such inferior courts as the Congress may from time to time ordain and establish. The judges, both of the Supreme and inferior courts, shall hold their offices during good behavior, and shall, at stated times, receive for their services a compensation which shall not be diminished during their continuance in office.

Article III skirts a complex subject by establishing a Supreme Court, sketching in only the most necessary of guidelines, and then delegating to Congress the authority to fill in the details.

Things to remember: Except for instances specified in Section 2, Paragraph 2, the Supreme Court is a court of *appellate* jurisdiction, taking cases only on appeal from other courts. An issue in *Marbury v. Madison*, perhaps the best known of all constitutional cases, hinged on jurisdiction (see Chapter 6, p. 95).

In 1975 Congress provided that judicial salaries would be periodically adjusted according to percentage increases granted other federal employees. Federal judges are paid considerably less than top corporation lawyers and the resulting turnover of lower court judges will be a growing concern in the bicentennial years. Salaries as of March, 1987: Chief Justice, $115,000; Associate Justices, $110,000; Federal Appeals Court Judges, $95,000; Federal District Judges, $95,000.

Section 2

Jurisdiction of Federal Courts.   1. The judicial power shall extend to all cases, in law and equity, arising under this Constitution, the laws of the United States, and treaties made, or which shall be made, under their authority; to all cases affecting ambassadors, other public ministers and consuls; to all cases of admiralty and maritime jurisdiction; to controversies to which the United States shall be a party; to controversies between two or more States; between a State and citizens of another State; between citizens of different States; between citizens of the same State claiming lands under grants of different States [and between a State, or the citizens thereof, and foreign states, citizens, or subjects.]

> The last fourteen words of Section 2, Paragraph 1 were abridged by the Eleventh Amendment. See 11th amendment, pp. 55-56.

Original and Appellate Jurisdiction of Supreme Court.   2. In all cases affecting ambassadors, other public ministers and consuls, and those in which a State shall be party, the Supreme Court shall have original jurisdiction. In all other cases before mentioned, the Supreme Court shall have appellate jurisdiction, both as to law and fact, with such exceptions, and under such regulations as the Congress shall make.

Trial of All Crimes, Except Impeachment, to Be by Jury.   3. The trial of all crimes, except in cases of impeachment, shall be by jury; and such trial shall be held in the State where the said crimes shall have been committed; but when not committed within any State, the trial shall be at such place or places as the Congress may by law have directed.

Section 3

Treason Defined; Conviction of.   1. Treason against the United States, shall consist only in levying war against them, or, in adhering to their enemies, giving them aid and comfort. No person shall be convicted of treason unless on the testimony of two witnesses to the same overt act, or on confession in open court.

> In the age of the hydrogen bomb and "Star Wars," treason becomes especially heinous. Revelation of classified information can nullify years of research and cost a nation billions of dollars—and perhaps even its existence. Note that such phrases as "levying war against them" (enemies), or, "in adhering to their enemies," or "giving them aid and comfort" are extremely broad. Do you think they should be redefined?

Congress to Declare Punishment for Treason.   2. The Congress shall have power to declare the punishment of treason, but no attainder of treason shall work corruption of blood, or forfeiture except during the life of the person attained.

Article IV—Federal-State Relations

Section 1

Each State to Give Full Faith and Credit to the Public Acts and Records of Other States. Full faith and credit shall be given in each State to the public acts, records, and judicial proceedings of every other State. And the Congress may by general laws prescribe the manner in which such acts, records and proceedings shall be proved, and the effect thereof.

Imagine the chaos that would follow if the marriages, divorces, and contracts executed in Georgia were not recognized in Utah or Maine! Article IV guards against such a possibility. The term "judicial proceedings" takes in all state laws and decrees. In some instances, a state may set certain minimum qualifications for acceptance of decrees of other states.

Professional licenses, being neither state laws nor edicts of a court, do not fall under the full faith and credit umbrella. Recognized state licensing and accrediting associations are free to set their own qualifications and to decide whether to make reciprocal arrangements. Thus Florida may guard against a winter influx of barbers (or beauty operators, lawyers, or CPAs) who might conceivably starve the resident professional workers and taxpayers.

Full faith and credit regulations *apply only to the states*, and *not* to other countries.

Section 2

Privileges of Citizens. 1. The citizens of each state shall be entitled to all privileges and immunities of citizens in the several States.

This assures fair treatment for visitors, traveling salesmen, out-of-state students, servicemen, etc. It also prohibits enactment of any statute that might, for instance, forbid out-of-staters from buying property. However, higher fees for visiting hunters and fishermen and higher tuition fees for out-of-state students attending state universities have been upheld.

Extradition between the Several States. 2. A person charged in any State with treason, felony, or other crime, who shall flee from justice, and be found in another State, shall on the demand of the executive authority of the State from which he fled, be delivered up, to be removed to the State having jurisdiction of the crime.

Without this clause a state might accept bribes, create a haven for fugitive criminals, and thwart the orderly criminal procedure of the nation.

Slaves. 3. No person held to service or labor in one State under the laws thereof, escaping into another, shall, in consequence of any law or regulation therein, be discharged from such service or labor, but shall be delivered up on claim of the party to whom such service or labor may be due.

This clause is outdated by the Thirteenth Amendment, ratified in 1865. See comment on the *Dred Scott* decision, Chapter 6, p. 102.

Section 3

New States. 1. New States may be admitted by the Congress into this Union; but no new State shall be formed or erected within the jurisdiction of any other State; nor any State be formed by junction of two or more States, or parts of States, without the consent of the Legislatures of the States concerned as well as of the Congress.

Congress controls admission of new states, but states already in the Union are assured of their lands. The Upper Peninsula of Michigan, far removed from Lansing in distance and philosophy, has often campaigned to be a separate state or to be joined with neighboring Wisconsin. Paragraph 1 requires approval by the state of Michigan and the United States Congress.

Regulations concerning Territory. 2. The Congress shall have power to dispose of and make all needful rules and regulations respecting the territory or other property belonging to the United States; and nothing in this Constitution shall be so construed as to prejudice any claims of the United States, or of any particular State.

The word "territory" refers to all outside lands over which the United States has jurisdiction, such as Puerto Rico. *Congress, not the president*, has final authority.

Section 4

Republican Form of Government and Protection Guaranteed the Several States. The United States shall guarantee to every State in this Union a Republican form of government, and shall protect each of them against invasion; and on application of the Legislature, or of the Executive (when the Legislature cannot be convened) against domestic violence.

A "Republican form of government" might be defined as one operated by properly representative delegates freely elected by the people. It would prohibit rule in any of the states by any king, emperor, dynasty, or hereditary ruler.

This is the only instance in the Constitution where the word "guarantee" is used. In the twentieth century many states have added such features as the initiative, the referendum, and the recall. These are *democratic* rather than *republican* (representative) actions.

Article V—The Amending Process

Ways in Which the Constitution Can Be Amended. The Congress, whenever two thirds of both Houses shall deem it necessary, shall propose amendments to this Constitution, or, on the application of the Legislatures of two thirds of the several States, shall call a convention for proposing amendments, which, in either case, shall be valid to all intents and purposes, as part of this Constitution, when ratified by the Legislatures of three fourths of the several States, or by conventions in three fourths thereof, as the one or the other mode of ratification may be proposed by the Congress; provided that no amendment which may be made prior to the year one thousand eight hundred and eight shall in any manner affect the first and fourth clauses in the Ninth Section of the First Article; and that no State, without its consent, shall be deprived of its equal suffrage in the Senate.

It's simpler than you think. For practical purposes, just remember: amendments are *proposed* by approval of two-thirds of both houses of Congress; *ratification* requires approval of three-fourths of the state legislatures.

Don't be too concerned with the alternative methods. They've practically never been used. No amendment has ever been proposed by the state legislatures. Of the first twenty-six amendments, only the Twenty-first was ratified by the convention method.

Presidents and governors have no official role in the amending process.

The Connecticut Compromise promised small states equal representation in the Senate. The last fifteen words of Article V seal that guarantee. This promise is absolute; it cannot be amended, except by consent, which will never be given.

For additional information on the amending process and on the individual amendments, see Chapter 4.

Article VI—Debts, National Supremacy, etc.

Debts Contracted under the Confederation Secured.   1. All debts contracted and engagements entered into, before the adoption of this Constitution, shall be as valid against the United States under this Constitution, as under the Confederation.

> Section 1 assures domestic and foreign creditors that the new nation, despite the treasury imbalance in excess of eighty million dollars, intends to discharge all commitments. In the family of nations, such notice was most impressive. American ambassadors would be more welcome, the country's treaty-making efforts would be met with greater respect, and its credit would be upgraded.

Constitution, Laws and Treaties of the United States to Be Supreme.   2. This Constitution, and the laws of the United States which shall be made in pursuance thereof; and all treaties made, or which shall be made, under the authority of the United States, shall be the supreme law of the land; and the judges in every State shall be bound thereby, any thing in the Constitution or laws of any State to the contrary notwithstanding.

> No more Articles of Confederation humbly making requests. Section 2 arms the new government with the kind of authority it will need to handle affairs at home and abroad. In ratifying the Constitution, each state will clearly understand that its actions must be sublimated to the "supreme law of the land."

Who Shall Take Constitutional Oaths; No Religious Test.   3. The Senators and Representatives before mentioned, and the members of the several State Legislatures, and all executive and judicial officers, both of the United States and of the several States, shall be bound by oath or affirmation, to support this Constitution; but no religious test shall ever be required as a qualification to any office or public trust under the United States.

> The first clause here often comes as a surprise to people who examine the Constitution, word for word, for the first time. Few realize that *state officials*, including judges, must take an oath to support the *federal* Constitution.
>
> The second clause does not forbid the *states* from requiring a religious test for state office. But the states, either by custom or constitutional provision, have conformed to the same proscription.

Article VII—Ratification

Ratification. The ratification of the Conventions of nine States shall be sufficient for the establishment of this Constitution between the States so ratifying the same.

> Last and least (in length) of the seven articles. Here again, the founders chose the republican form, requiring approval by representatives gathered in special state conventions where conditions favored the Federalists (see Chapter 3).
>
> Many scholars believe that the Constitution would not have been approved by a simple majority of qualified voters.

Done in Convention by the Unanimous Consent of the States present the Seventeenth Day of September in the Year of our Lord one thousand seven hundred and Eighty seven and of the Independence of the United States of America the Twelfth. In Witness whereof We have hereunto subscribed our Names.

G⁰. WASHINGTON
President and Deputy from Virginia

New Hampshire.
John Langdon
Nicholas Gilman

Massachusetts.
Nathaniel Gorham
Rufus King

Connecticut.
Wm. Saml. Johnson
Roger Sherman

New York.
Alexander Hamilton

New Jersey.
Wil: Livingston
David Brearley
Wm. Patterson
Jona: Dayton

Pennsylvania.
B. Franklin
Robt. Morris
Thos. Fitzsimmons
James Wilson

Thomas Mifflin
Geo. Clymer
Jared Ingersoll
Gouv. Morris

Delaware.
Geo: Reed
John Dickinson
Jaco: Broom
Gunning Bedford Jun
Richard Bassett

Maryland.
James McHenry
Danl. Carroll
Dan: of St. Thos. Jenifer

Virginia.
John Blair
James Madison, Jr.

North Carolina.
Wm. Blount
Hu. Williamson
Richd. Dobbs Spaight

South Carolina.

J. Rutledge
Charles Pinckney
Charles Cotesworth Pinckney
Pierce Butler

Georgia.

William Few
Abr. Baldwin

Attest: WILLIAM JACKSON, *Secretary*

QUESTIONS

1. Why does the Constitution first deal with powers of the House of Representatives?
2. Which branch of Congress decides upon impeachment and which branch conducts the impeachment trial?
3. Who presides at the impeachment trial of a president?
4. How can a presidential veto be overridden?
5. Could Gerald Ford have pardoned Richard Nixon if he had been convicted in impeachment proceedings?
6. What is the minimum age for a president?
7. Does the president have sole power to make treaties?
8. Only a *natural born* citizen can become president today, a provision that would bar Henry Kissinger, who served as Secretary of State under Presidents Nixon and Ford. Would that same provision have kept West Indian-born Alexander Hamilton or Swiss-born Albert Gallatin, Jefferson's Secretary of the Treasury, from being president?
9. Why does Article II, Section 4 provide that the president can receive neither a raise nor a salary cut during his term?
10. Does a civil officer who has been impeached and convicted have the right of appeal?
11. Why did President Reagan receive no increase in salary in 1987 when the vice-president, members of Congress and all federal judges received raises?
12. Why does the veto power appear in Article I rather than in Article II, the Executive Article?

See Answers to Questions, pp. 175–76.

Fill in the Blanks (Answers are on p. 176.)

1. Members of the House of Representatives are chosen every _____ years.
2. A Representative must reside in the state in which he or she is chosen, have been a citizen _____ years, and be _____ years old.

3. A U.S. Senator must be _____ years of age and _____ years a citizen.

4. The Senate is presided over by the _____ _____.

5. The president of the Senate may vote only in case of a _____.

6. The sole power of impeachment rests with the _____, and the power to try impeachment lies with the _____.

7. In case of impeachment of the president, the _____ _____ shall preside at the trial.

8. When a vacancy occurs in the Senate, the _____ _____ appoints someone to fill the office until the next general election.

9. When a vacancy occurs in the House, the _____ _____ issues a _____ _____ _____.

10. All revenue-raising bills originate in the _____.

11. Only the _____ has the power to negotiate a treaty. But a treaty, to become law, must be approved by a _____ vote of the _____.

12. The power to appoint ambassadors and Supreme Court justices is vested in the _____.

Multiple Choice

_____ 13. Which one of these powers does NOT belong to the Congress:
   a. To lay and collect taxes
   b. to establish post offices
   c. to interpret the laws
   d. to provide and maintain a navy
   e. to issue patents
   f. to coin money
   g. to declare war

_____ 14. An impeached government official is NOT subject to which of these penalties as a result of impeachment:
   a. removal from office
   b. fine and imprisonment
   c. disqualification from holding further federal offices

_____ 15. Which of these crimes is defined in the Constitution?
   a. malfeasance in office
   b. treason
   c. perjury
   d. misappropriation of funds

_____ 16. A federal judge serves for:
   a. 6 years
   b. 4 years

     c. life

     d. 10 years

     e. until age 70

_____ 17. The principle of judicial review was established in:

     a. *Cohens* v. *Virginia*

     b. *Brown* v. *Board of Education*

     c. *Marbury* v. *Madison*

     d. *Nixon* v. *Jaworski*

_____ 18. The federal government must guarantee to each state which kind of government?

     a. democratic

     b. republican

     c. popular

     d. representative

_____ 19. Article V provides that amendments may be ratified by conventions called by the state legislatures. How many amendments have been ratified in this manner?

     a. 4

     b. 22

     c. none

     d. 1

     e. 8

     f. 25

_____ 20. To become law, an amendment must be ratified by:

     a. two-thirds of the states

     b. the Congress, and signed by the president

     c. three-fourths of the state legislatures

_____ 21. Article VI provided that all obligations contracted by the Articles of Confederation government:

     a. would be paid in full

     b. were not necessarily the obligation of the new government

     c. would be paid if approved by the Congress and signed by the president

_____ 22. Which of the following is not listed in Article VI as being among the rules which comprise the supreme law of the land?

     a. Constitution

     b. executive proclamations

     c. treaties

     d. laws of the U.S.

_____ 23. Which of the following acts is not defined as treasonous?
   a. levying war against the U.S.
   b. adhering to the enemies of the U.S.
   c. "Bugging" the halls of Congress
   d. giving aid and comfort to the enemy

_____ 24. Article VI provided that the Constitution, to become law, must be ratified by how many states?
   a. 7
   b. 13
   c. 9
   d. 8

_____ 25. Which one of the following was not provided in Article IV?
   a. each state must honor the public acts, records and judicial proceedings of every other state.
   b. citizens of any state are entitled to the privileges of citizens of all the states.
   c. states must turn over captured criminals who are wanted in other states.
   d. states must not harbor runaway slaves from another state.
   e. in time of war, states may restrict out-of-state traffic on their roads and waterways.

_____ 26. Jack Kemp and Mario Cuomo could not run on the same ticket for president and vice-president because:
   a. Kemp is a Republican and Cuomo is a Democrat.
   b. both are from the same state.
   c. Article II provides that a presidential candidate from the east must have a running mate from another section of the country.

_____ 27. Carmelita Gomez, a Mexican citizen who illegally entered the United States to work and live in a Texas border town, bears a child out of wedlock. The child, according to the Fourteenth Amendment, is therefore:
   a. A full-fledged U.S. citizen.
   b. considered an alien.
   c. possessed of half citizenship if it can be proved the father was a U.S. citizen.

Introduction to the Declaration of Independence

"MOST NOBLE DOCUMENT EVER CONCEIVED BY THE MIND OF MAN"

The city of Quebec in 1759 was a natural fortress fashioned by God, reinforced by the French, and garrisoned by the troops of the Marquis de Montcalm. From his command post on the Plains of Abraham, high above the city, the intrepid Montcalm could look down upon the St. Lawrence Valley and smile with a comfort born of military wisdom. From this superb tactical position, his defending French forces were secure from any threat of the British General James Wolfe, whose forces numbered about 7,000.

But the 33 year old British commander apparently did not understand the meaning of the word "impossible." Under cover of darkness his boats slithered 3,600 men down the St. Lawrence to a point from which they would be able to negotiate the rugged ascent to the Plains. At daybreak on September 13 the French awakened to find the Wolfe at their doorstep. In the fierce fighting, which raged for several days, both generals lost their lives. Montcalm's last hours were rendered even more bitter by the sense of impending defeat; Wolfe's were comforted in the radiance of historic victory.

The fall of Quebec City was the climax of the French and Indian War. A few weeks later Admiral Hawke destroyed a large French fleet off the coast of Brittany; Montreal would fall within 12 months. The French menace in America was forever eradicated.

The French and Indian War in the New World was but a sideshow in the global Seven Years War (1756–63) which climaxed the century-long confrontation between two rising European powers—France and England. The struggle for dominion in Africa would simmer into the 19th century. On the European front, Prussia's Frederick the Great, bankrolled by his English allies, delivered devastating blows to the French land forces. In India, the legendary Robert Clive spearheaded a drive for English hegemony. His brilliant military triumph in 1757 gave the English mastery of Bengal; Pondicherry, the French capital in India, crumbled in 1761. Between his unsuccessful suicide attempt as a teenager and his successful attempt as a middle-age man, the clerk who had no formal military experience had conquered one of the most lucrative empires in world history.

Her status as an international commercial power severely dimmed, her ships swept from the high seas, her African visions frustrated, her colonial empires in America and India destroyed, her land forces humiliated at home, her treasury emptied, France came out of the Seven Years War and the calamitous Treaty of Paris of 1763 with a bitterness toward England that was as deep as the Channel which separated the two neighbors.

It was a venom which would soon steer the rudder of history. For it was consuming contempt for the British more than friendship for America which motivated the bankrupt and downtrodden French to provide the critical arms and supplies which 20 years later would prove decisive in America's War of Independence.

Our forefathers' disenchantment with the mother country intensified shortly after the French threat was dispelled. How natural, thought George III and his Parliament, that Americans be asked to defray some of the wartime expenses and part of the continuing cost of maintaining British soldiers to keep the peace along the Ohio Valley. In arbitrarily imposing taxes for these purposes, the English incited the first successful revolution in the history of modern Western Civilization.

George III, Lord North, Lord Townshend, the Stamp Act, the Intolerable Acts, the Stamp Act Congress, the Declaratory Act, the Sugar Act, the Writs of Assistance, the Boston Tea Party, the Continental Congress, Concord, Lexington, Minute Men, *Common Sense,* the midnight ride of Paul Revere, "give me liberty or give me death" and "taxation without representation is tyranny": these are but a few of the familiar notes in the overture that introduced the Declaration of Independence to center stage in world history. They were notes orchestrated in the stirring, quickstep years from the fall of Quebec (1759) to that Fourth Day of July 1776, when a new nation would forsake the womb of the mother country and take its first shaky steps on its own.

It was to this pulsing background that Richard Henry Lee a delegate from Virginia rose in the Second Continental Congress on June 7, 1776, and proposed three resolutions, the first of which pronounced that:

> these United Colonies are, and of right ought to be, free and independent
> States, that they are absolved from all allegiance to the British Crown,

and that all political connection between them and the State of Great Britain is, and ought to be, totally dissolved.

Several of the state delegations believed they were without authority to cast votes on such a crucial question, and a postponement of several weeks was agreed upon. Three days later the Congress voted to appoint a committee to prepare a statement of reasons for such a breakaway, to be announced to the world in the event Congress passed the resolution of the honorable gentleman from Virginia. The following day, June 11, a committee was named, consisting of Thomas Jefferson, John Adams, Benjamin Franklin, Roger Sherman, and Robert Livingston.

The task of authorship providentially fell upon Thomas Jefferson, "the man whom God would have selected to compose the Sermon on the Mount, had he been around at the time." Aristocratic yet democratic, firm but tolerant, possessed of the mind of a scholar and the heart of a humanist, the tall, ruddy, 33-year-old Virginia scholar was a masterful choice to translate into clear, logical perspective the spirit of rebellion, the wisdom of the *philosophes,* and the mortal sins of George III.

Lawyer, assemblyman, congressman, violinist, horseman, architect, inventor, educator, writer, country squire, patron of art, Jefferson had an enthusiasm for literature, political science, geology, zoology, medicine, and aeronautics that was matched by an intense lifelong interest in democracy, the common welfare, human rights, and dignity. He was not new to the job. From his sickbed he had drafted Virginia's defiant reply to Lord North's "propositions." In 1775, as a congressman, he wrote Congress' answer to those same propositions, as well as the Congressional "Declaration of the Causes and Necessity for Taking up Arms." He also was author of a pamphlet, *A Summary View of the Rights of Americans* (1774), in which he posed cogent historical precedents which questioned the English Parliament's legal claim to authority over colonial America.

The record shows that this flaming interest in basic constitutional rights did not dim after July 4, 1776. In 1788, while serving as minister to France, his would be one of the most strident voices insisting upon a Bill of Rights to accompany the Constitution. Twenty-two years after the Declaration of Independence was adopted, Jefferson would be in the forefront of the fight to repeal the freedom-destroying Alien and Sedition Acts. In this campaign the two most effective instruments were the Virginia and Kentucky Resolutions. He lent his prestige to adoption of the Virginia Resolutions and was author of the Kentucky Resolutions. No man in America was better fitted, philosophically and intellectually, to write the "most noble document ever conceived by the mind of man."

Working long hours at the portable folding desk which he himself had designed (and which is now on display at the National Museum, Washington), Jefferson came up with an initial draft which he submitted to Adams and

Franklin. After incorporating their suggestions for changes, he presented the statement (the word "Declaration" was never used by Jefferson at that time) to the committee, which recommended further amendments. On June 28 the committee submitted the approval draft to the Continental Congress, which in turn insisted on numerous modifications. To Jefferson, the most distasteful of these was the deletion of the statement condemning the slave trade.

Richard Henry Lee's Resolution of Independence was adopted by Congress on July 2, 1776, a day that might logically have been designated as the birthday of our Republic.

But History had its eye on another day and a more stirring document. On July 4 the Congress approved Jefferson's statement of the reasons compelling the colonists to adopt Lee's Resolution. It was this statement that was later christened the Declaration of Independence.

An historic document, the English Bill of Rights, and a famous political tract, John Locke's *Second Treatise of Government,* were Jefferson's primary sources for the Declaration of Independence.

In 1688, fearing a Catholic succession, the Whigs accomplished their Glorious Revolution, overthrowing James II and bringing William of Orange and Mary (James' Protestant daughter by a first marriage) to the English throne. In consequence of this, the world-famous Bill of Rights was adopted the following year, guaranteeing the Protestant succession for all time, listing basic constitutional rights, and detailing the charges against James II.

The causes which prompted the Whigs to rebel against James Stuart in 1688 were much the same as those which motivated the American colonists to revolt against George III a century later. Jefferson pounced on this remarkable political parallel. His litany of accusations against George III are in the same vein as the 13 charges which the English made against their own king shortly after they forced him to flee to France, tossing the Great Seal in the Thames on his escape to safety. "By God, they are paddling us with our own belt straps," remarked one of the Lords in Parliament upon reading the American Declaration of Independence. It is interesting to note that Jefferson fixed total blame upon George III. The word "Parliament" is never mentioned in the Declaration.

Chief political and philosophical apologist for the English action in dethroning James II was John Locke, 1632–1704, whose first and second *Treatises of Government* (1690) were written to justify the Glorious Revolution. His theories of a "compact system of government," of a "social contract," and of the "right to rebellion," detailed in *The Second Treatise of Government,* were copied by Jefferson in the Declaration of Independence.

Men enter the world totally free, according to Locke. They are unfettered by any chains of authority and endowed by their Creator with such "natural" rights as life, liberty, and property. But because of the imperfections of man, the state of total serenity and security in nature is not attainable without a few "ground rules." Thus, men voluntarily surrender a part of their freedom in order to protect their lives and possessions. By agreement (or compact) they choose a way of government headed by one of their own. When this compact is broken, the people have not only the right, but the *duty,* to rebel.

James' real sin was having produced a son (the unquestioned heir apparent to the English throne) by his Catholic wife. His official sin was "having endeavoured to subvert the constitution of the kingdom by breaking the original contract between king and people, and having, by the advice of Jesuits and other wicked persons, violated the fundamental laws. . . ."

Theorists also read into the Declaration the "social contract" ideas of Rousseau, the "natural law" doctrines of Aquinas and other medievalists, the admonitions of Thomas Paine as expressed in *Common Sense,* and some of the thinking of Montesquieu, Grotius, and even Plato. Although the sage of Monticello was familiar with the works of all these men, and others, John Locke remains the philosophical seed from which the Declaration of Independence sprouted.

Although reference in this chapter is primarily to the English revolt of 1688, it must be remembered that the first 60 years of the 17th century was a running chronicle of the constitutional conflict which raged between crown and Parliament in England. Many of the constitutional points brought home by Jefferson and others in the 1770s were the same as those propounded by Sir Edmund Coke, John Pym, John Hampden, John Milton, and by Oliver Cromwell and his Roundheads as they sent Charles II to his eternal reward in 1649.

There are three "official" texts of the Declaration—the "rough draft," the "corrected" version, and the familiar copy, engrossed on parchment with the signatures, headed by the bold autograph of John Hancock.

The "rough draft" broadside was printed by John Dunlap of Philadelphia a few hours after the Declaration was approved. This is the text first authorized to be printed by Congress and the one inserted in the "rough" Journal of Congress.

The "corrected" text is in the handwriting of Charles Thomson, secretary of Congress, and is placed in the "corrected" Journal of Congress.

Both of these texts are preserved in the papers of the Continental Congress in the Library of Congress.

The parchment copy, preserved in a helium-filled glass, is the familiar one displayed in countless photographs and viewed annually by millions of visitors who throng the National Archives Building in Washington, D.C.

The first celebration of the Declaration of Independence took place July 8, 1776, at Independence Hall (known then as the state house). The celebrators were summoned for a reading by the pealing of the Liberty Bell. The story that the Liberty Bell first cracked on that day has been widely circulated, but is untrue. It cracked for the first time in 1752 after being brought from London.

In the annals of world history, few documents have had such enormous influence. The words of the Declaration of Independence were the inspiration for

French patriots who revolted against 200 years of Bourbon oppression in 1789 to proclaim their own *Declaration of the Rights of Man and of the Citizen.* In the years from 1789 to 1848 numerous revolutionary movements erupted throughout Europe; between 1810 and 1825 virtually every country in South America rose in protest. Wherever men have risked their lives to rid themselves of the burden of unjust government, Jefferson's ringing statement of America's revolutionary rationale has stood out like a beacon of hope in the canyon of royal absolutism.

Thomas Jefferson died on July 4, 1826, at Monticello on the golden anniversary of the Declaration of Independence, within hours of the death of another great patriot, John Adams. Thus, the bicentennial anniversary of the Declaration of Independence will fall on the sesquicentennial anniversary of the death of Adams and Jefferson.

THE DECLARATION OF INDEPENDENCE

In CONGRESS, July 4, 1776
A DECLARATION
By the REPRESENTATIVES of the
UNITED STATES OF AMERICA
In GENERAL CONGRESS assembled

When in the Course of human Events, it becomes necessary for one People to dissolve the Political Bands which have connected them with another, and to assume among the Powers of the Earth, the separate and equal Station to which the Laws of Nature and of Nature's God entitle them, a decent Respect to the Opinions of Mankind requires that they should declare the causes which impel them to the Separation.

We hold these Truths to be self-evident, that all Men are created equal, that they are endowed by their Creator with certain unalienable Rights, that among these are Life, Liberty, and the Pursuit of Happiness—That to secure these Rights, Governments are instituted among Men, deriving their just Powers from the Consent of the Governed, that whenever any Form of Government becomes destructive of these Ends, it is the Right of the People to alter or to abolish it, and to institute new Government, laying its Foundation on such Principles, and organizing its Powers in such Form, as to them shall seem most

---

Text and notes as found in *The Declaration of Independence and The Constitution of the United States of America* (Washington, D.C.: House of Representatives, 1964), pp. 1–5.

likely to effect their Safety and Happiness. Prudence, indeed, will dictate that Governments long established should not be changed for light and transient Causes; and accordingly all Experience hath shewn, that Mankind are more disposed to suffer, while Evils are sufferable, than to right themselves by abolishing the Forms to which they are accustomed. But when a long Train of Abuses and Usurpations, pursuing invariably the same Object, evinces a Design to reduce them under absolute Despotism, it is their Right, it is their duty, to throw off such government, and to provide new Guards for their future Security. Such has been the patient Sufferance of these Colonies; and such is now the Necessity which constrains them to alter their former Systems of Government. The History of the present King of Great-Britain is a History of repeated Injuries and Usurpations, all having in direct Object the Establishment of an absolute Tyranny over these States. To prove this, let Facts be submitted to a candid World.

He has refused his Assent to Laws, the most wholesome and necessary for the public Good.

He has forbidden his Governors to pass Laws of immediate and pressing Importance, unless suspended in their Operation till his Assent should be obtained; and when so suspended, he has utterly neglected to attend to them.

He has refused to pass other Laws for the Accommodation of large Districts of People, unless those People would relinquish the Right of Representation in the Legislature, a Right inestimable to them, and formidable to Tyrants only.

He has called together Legislative Bodies at Places unusual, uncomfortable, and distant from the Depository of their public Records, for the sole Purpose of fatiguing them into Compliance with his Measures.

He has dissolved Representative Houses repeatedly, for opposing with manly Firmness his Invasions on the Rights of the People.

He has refused for a long Time, after such Dissolutions, to cause others to be elected; whereby the Legislative Powers, incapable of Annihilation, have returned to the People at large for their exercise; the State remaining in the mean time exposed to all the Dangers of Invasion from without, and Convulsions within.

He has endeavoured to prevent the Population of these States; for that Purpose obstructing the Laws for Naturalization of Foreigners; refusing to pass others to encourage their Migrations hither, and raising the Conditions of new Appropriations of Lands.

He has obstructed the Administration of Justice, by refusing his Assent to Laws for establishing Judiciary Powers.

He has made Judges dependent on his Will alone, for the Tenure of their Offices, and the Amount and Payment of their Salaries.

He has erected a Multitude of new Offices, and sent hither Swarms of Officers to harrass our People, and eat out their Substance.

He has kept among us, in Times of Peace, Standing Armies, without the consent of our Legislatures.

He has affected to render the Military independent of and superior to the Civil Power.

He has combined with others to subject us to a Jurisdiction foreign to our Constitution, and unacknowledged by our Laws; giving his Assent to their Acts of pretended Legislation:

For quartering large Bodies of Armed Troops among us:

For protecting them, by a mock Trial, from Punishment for any Murders which they should commit on the Inhabitants of these States:

For cutting off our Trade with all Parts of the World:

For imposing Taxes on us without our Consent:

For depriving us, in many Cases, of the Benefits of Trial by Jury:

For transporting us beyond Seas to be tried for pretended Offences:

For abolishing the free System of English Laws in a neighboring Province, establishing therein an arbitrary Government, and enlarging its Boundaries, so as to render it at once an Example and fit Instrument for introducing the same absolute Rule into these Colonies:

For taking away our Charters, abolishing our most valuable Laws, and altering fundamentally the Forms of our Governments:

For suspending our own Legislatures, and declaring themselves invested with Power to legislate for us in all Cases whatsoever.

He has abdicated Government here, by declaring us out of his Protection and waging War against us.

He has plundered our Seas, ravaged our Coasts, burnt our Towns, and destroyed the Lives of our People.

He is, at this Time, transporting large Armies of foreign Mercenaries to compleat the Works of Death, Desolation, and Tyranny, already begun with circumstances of Cruelty and Perfidy, scarcely paralleled in the most barbarous Ages, and totally unworthy the Head of a civilized Nation.

He has constrained our fellow Citizens taken Captive on the high Seas to bear Arms against their Country, to become the Executioners of their Friends and Brethren, or to fall themselves at their Hands.

He has excited domestic Insurrections amongst us, and has endeavoured to bring on the Inhabitants of our Frontiers, the merciless Indian Savages, whose known Rule of Warfare, is an undistinguished Destruction, of all Ages, Sexes and Conditions.

In every stage of these Oppressions we have Petitioned for Redress in the most humble Terms: Our repeated Petitions have been answered only by repeated Injury. A Prince, whose Character is thus marked by every act which may define a Tyrant, is unfit to be the Ruler of a free People.

Nor have we been wanting in Attentions to our British Brethren. We have warned them from Time to Time of Attempts by their Legislature to extend an unwarrantable Jurisdiction over us. We have reminded them of the Circumstances of our Emigration and Settlement here. We have appealed to their native Justice and Magnanimity, and we have conjured them by the Ties of our common Kindred to disavow these Usurpations, which, would inevitably interrupt our Connections and Correspondence. They too have been deaf to the Voice of Justice and of Consanguinity. We must, therefore, acquiesce in the Necessity, which denounces our Separation and hold them, as we hold the rest of Mankind, Enemies in War, in Peace, Friends.

We, therefore, the Representatives of the UNITED STATES OF AMERICA, in GENERAL CONGRESS, Assembled, appealing to the Supreme Judge of the World for the Rectitude of our Intentions, do, in the Name, and by Authority of the good People of these Colonies, solemnly Publish and Declare, That these United Colonies are, and of Right ought to be, FREE AND INDEPENDENT STATES; that they are absolved from all Allegiance to the British Crown, and that all political Connection between them and the State of Great-Britain, is and ought to be totally dissolved; and that as FREE AND INDEPENDENT STATES, they have full Power to levy War, conclude Peace, contract Alliances, establish Commerce, and to do all other Acts and Things which INDEPENDENT STATES may of right do. And for the support of this Declaration, with a firm Reliance on the Protection of divine Providence, we mutually pledge to each other our Lives, our Fortunes, and our sacred Honor.

Signed by ORDER *and in* BEHALF *of the* CONGRESS,
JOHN HANCOCK, PRESIDENT.

ATTEST.
CHARLES THOMSON, SECRETARY.

PHILADELPHIA: PRINTED BY JOHN DUNLAP.

SIGNERS OF THE DECLARATION OF INDEPENDENCE

*ACCORDING TO THE AUTHENTICATED LIST PRINTED BY
ORDER OF CONGRESS OF JANUARY 18, 1777**

John Hancock

New-Hampshire.

Josiah Bartlett,
Wm. Whipple,
Matthew Thornton. †

Massachusetts-Bay.

Saml. Adams,
John Adams,

Robt. Treat Paine,
Elbridge Gerry.

Rhode-Island and Providence, &C.

Step. Hopkins,
William Ellery.

Connecticut.

Roger Sherman,
Saml. Huntington,

---

*Spelling and abbreviation of names conform to original printed list.

†Matthew Thornton's name was signed on the engrossed copy following the Connecticut Members, but was transferred in the printed copy to its proper place with the other New Hampshire Members.

Wm. Williams,
Oliver Wolcott.

New-York.

Wm. Floyd,
Phil. Livingston,
Frans. Lewis,
Lewis Morris.

New-Jersey.

Richd. Stockton,
Jno. Witherspoon,
Fras. Hopkinson,
John Hart,
Abra. Clark.

Pennsylvania.

Robt. Morris,
Benjamin Rush,
Benja. Franklin,
John Morton,
Geo. Clymer,
Jas. Smith,
Geo. Taylor,
James Wilson,
Geo. Ross.

Delaware.

Caesar Rodney,
Geo. Read,
(Tho M:Kean.)‡

Maryland.

Samuel Chase,
Wm. Paca,
Thos. Stone,
Charles Carroll, of Carrollton.

Virginia.

George Wythe,
Richard Henry Lee,
Ths. Jefferson,
Benja. Harrison,
Thos. Nelson, Jr.
Francis Lightfoot Lee,
Carter Braxton.

North-Carolina.

Wm. Hooper,
Joseph Hewes,
John Penn.

South-Carolina.

Edward Rutledge,
Thos. Heyward, junr.
Thomas Lynch, junr.
Arthur Middleton.

Georgia.

Button Gwinnett,
Lyman Hall,
Geo. Walton.

---

‡Thomas McKean's name was not included in the list of signers printed by order of Congress on January 18, 1777, as he did not sign the engrossed copy until some time thereafter, probably in 1781.

B

Articles of Confederation

INTRODUCTION

A backdrop of bitterness, fear, and suspicion clouds the phraseology and philosophy of the Articles of Confederation. Forged in the flames of war, the document is dominated by a fierce resolve to cling to a local type of autonomy but tempered by a grudging realization that it is better to hang together than to hang separately.

In July of 1775, while the memory of Concord and Lexington was still fresh, Benjamin Franklin proposed to the Continental Congress a plan for "Articles of Confederation and Perpetual Union." But Franklin's "firm league of friendship" was dismissed; the colonists were not yet ready to grant to any government—even one of their own formation—a slice of that political independence which many of them would soon defend with their lives.

On June 7, 1777, Richard Henry Lee's resolution for a Declaration of Independence was accompanied by a resolution that Congress consider a written constitution. The move carried and John Dickenson headed the committee which reported back on July 12. Conflicts instantly flared between small-states people and large-states people, between nationalists and localists, between idealists and realists.

Dickenson's much debated and embroidered Articles of Confederation were submitted to the states in November 1777, at the beginning of the winter of Valley Forge. Twelve states ratified within two years, but a lone dissenter held up the necessary unanimous approval for another two years. Maryland was disturbed by the claims of seven states—claims which in some cases stretched to the Mississippi and in others lengthened to the Pacific. Only when all claims were ceded to the United States did Maryland ratify the Articles and make them the law of the land. In many respects the document merely gave legal, written sanction to a form of government which had been in existence for several years.

The Articles of Confederation, of course, are best known for what they failed to say. Note the absence of a federal judiciary, the lack of a federal taxing authority, the failure to grant the government the power to create its own army or to regulate commerce, and the cavernous void brought about by refusal to name an executive.

Missing also are the graceful prose and simple clarity of the United States Constitution; nor is there any hint of the poetic cadence with which Thomas Jefferson endowed the Declaration of Independence. Details of the various Articles are ponderously qualified, and verbs have a habit of straying word-miles away from their nouns. We challenge the reader, within a 30 minute time limitation, to come up with a meaningful translation of the second sentence of the second paragraph of Article Nine.

ARTICLES OF CONFEDERATION

To ALL to whom these Presents shall come, we the undersigned Delegates of the States affixed to our Names send greeting.

Whereas the Delegates of the United States of America in Congress assembled did on the fifteenth day of November in the Year of our Lord One Thousand Seven Hundred and Seventy seven, and in the Second Year of the Independence of America agree to certain articles of Confederation and perpetual Union between the States of Newhampshire, Massachusetts-bay, Rhodeisland and Providence Plantations, Connecticut, New York, New Jersey, Pennsylvania, Delaware, Maryland, Virginia, North-Carolina, South-Carolina and Georgia in the Words following, viz.

Articles of Confederation and perpetual Union between the States of Newhampshire, Massachusetts-bay, Rhodeisland and Providence Plantations, Connecticut, New-York, New-Jersey, Pennsylvania, Delaware, Maryland, Virginia, North-Carolina, South-Carolina and Georgia.

Article I

The stile of this confederacy shall be "The United States of America."

Article II

Each State retains its sovereignty, freedom, and independence, and every power, jurisdiction and right, which is not by this confederation expressly delegated to the United States, in Congress assembled.

This Article, a total victory for the states' rights faction, sets the pattern for the entire document. Clearly, the majority wished to guard against a strong central government. If they were successful in breaking away from the authority of George III and Parliament, they meant to insure they would never again be so dominated.

Article III

The said States hereby severally enter into a firm league of friendship with each other, for their common defence, the security of their liberties, and their mutual and general welfare, binding themselves to assist each other, against all force offered to, or attacks made upon them, or any of them, on account of religion, sovereignty, trade, or any other pretence whatever.

Note the terms *firm league of friendship, common defence,* and *security of their liberties.* Following the tone struck in Article II, Article III's statement of purpose indicates that the Articles of Confederation were conceived primarily as a mutual alliance in the fight against England. As much autonomy as possible would be reserved for the individual states.

Article IV

The better to secure and perpetuate mutual friendship and intercourse among the people of the different States in this Union, the free inhabitants of each of these States, paupers, vagabonds and fugitives from justice excepted, shall be entitled to all privileges and immunities of free citizens in the several States; and the people of each State shall have free ingress and regress to and from any other State, and shall enjoy therein all the privileges of trade and commerce, subject to the same duties, impositions and restrictions as the inhabitants thereof respectively, provided that such restrictions shall not extend so far as to prevent the removal of property imported into any State, to any other State of which the owner is an inhabitant; provided also that no imposition, duties, or restriction shall be laid by any State, on the property of the United States, or either of them.

If any person guilty of, or charged with treason, felony, or other high misdemeanor in any State, shall flee from justice, and be found in any of the United States, he shall upon demand of the Governor or Executive power, of the State from which he fled, be delivered up and removed to the State having jurisdiction of his offence.

Full faith and credit shall be given in each of these States to the records, acts and judicial proceedings of the courts and magistrates of every other State.

> Some are more equal than others.
>
> States were free to impose duties on interstate commerce. A windfall for New York. (One of the main faults of the Articles.)
>
> Paragraph 3 was lifted almost verbatim by the authors of the Constitution. In both documents, extradition and full faith and credit are dealt with in Article IV.

Article V

For the more convenient management of the general interests of the United States, delegates shall be annually appointed in such manner as the legislature of each State shall direct, to meet in Congress on the first Monday in November, in every year, with a power reserved to each State, to recall its delegates, or any of them, at any time within the year, and to send others in their stead, for the remainder of the year.

No State shall be represented in Congress by less than two, nor by more than seven members; and no person shall be capable of being a delegate for more than three years in any term of six years; nor shall any person, being a delegate, be capable of holding any office under the United States, for which he, or another for his benefit receives any salary, fees or emolument of any kind.

Each State shall maintain its own delegates in a meeting of the States, and while they act as members of the committee of the States.

In determining questions in the United States, in Congress assembled, each State shall have one vote.

Freedom of speech and debate in Congress shall not be impeached or questioned in any court, or place out of Congress, and the members of Congress shall be protected in their persons from arrests and imprisonments, during the time of their going to and from, and attendance on Congress, except for treason, felony, or breach of peace.

> Note: A *single* legislative branch; members appointed *annually* with each state free to select the manner in which delegates would be chosen. Annual appointments reflected the colonists revulsion against a

House-of-Lords-type rule where peers were elected for life.
Paragraph 2. Since the states paid the delegates, each state could have as many as it wished; however, each state got only one vote.
Again, the Articles carefully guard against long terms of office.
Paragraph 4. Total victory for the small states. Delaware could exert the same power as Massachusetts or Pennsylvania.

Article VI

No State without the consent of the United States in Congress assembled, shall send any embassy to, or receive any embassy from, or enter into any conference, agreement, alliance or treaty with any king, prince or state; nor shall any person holding any office of profit or trust under the United States, or any of them, accept of any present, emolument, office or title of any kind whatever from any king, prince or foreign state; nor shall the United States in Congress assembled, or any of them, grant any title of nobility.

No two or more States shall enter into any treaty, confederation or alliance whatever between them, without the consent of the United States in Congress assembled, specifying accurately the purposes for which the same is to be entered into, and how long it shall continue.

No State shall lay any imposts or duties, which may interfere with any stipulations in treaties, entered into by the United States in Congress assembled, with any king, prince or state, in pursuance of any treaties already proposed by Congress, to the courts of France and Spain.

No vessels of war shall be kept up in time of peace by any State, except such number only, as shall be deemed necessary by the United States in Congress assembled, for the defence of such State, or its trade; nor shall any body of forces be kept up by any State, in time of peace, except such number only, as in the judgment of the United States, in Congress assembled, shall be deemed requisite to garrison the forts necessary for the defence of such State; but every State shall always keep up a well regulated and disciplined militia, sufficiently armed and accoutred, and shall provide and constantly have ready for use, in public stores, a due number of field pieces and tents, and a proper quantity of arms, ammunition and camp equipage.

No State shall engage in any war without the consent of the United States in Congress assembed, unless such State be actually invaded by enemies, or shall have received certain advice of a resolution being formed by some nation of Indians to invade such State, and the danger is so imminent as not to admit of a delay, till the United States in Congress assembled can be consulted: nor shall any State grant commissions to any ships or vessels of war, nor letters of marque or reprisal, except it be after a declaration of war by the United States in Congress assembled, and then only against the kingdom or state and the subjects thereof, against which war has been so declared, and under such regulations as shall be established by the United States in Congress assembled, unless such State be infested by pirates, in which case vessels of war may be fitted out for that occasion, and kept so long as the danger shall continue, or until the United States in Congress assembled shall determine otherwise.

Article VII

When land-forces are raised by any State for the common defence, all officers of or under the rank of colonel, shall be appointed by the Legislature of each State respectively by whom such forces shall be raised, or in such manner as such State shall direct, and all vacancies shall be filled up by the State which first made the appointment.

> Prohibitions on the states.
> *Paragraph 1.* Expressing a common revulsion against the British system.

Article VIII

All charges of war, and all other expenses that shall be incurred for the common defence or general welfare, and allowed by the United States in Congress assembled, shall be defrayed out of a common treasury, which shall be supplied by the several States, in proportion to the value of all land within each State, granted to or surveyed for any person, as such land and the buildings and improvements thereon shall be estimated according to such mode as the United States in Congress assembled, shall from time to time direct and appoint.

The taxes for paying that proportion shall be laid and levied by the authority and direction of the Legislatures of the several States within the time agreed upon by the United States in Congress assembled.

> The good intentions expressed in Articles VII and VIII are nullified by this ambiguous and unenforceable clause. Again, the individual state legislatures exerted enormous power.

Article IX

The United States in Congress assembled, shall have the sole and exclusive right and power of determining on peace and war, except in the cases mentioned in the sixth article—of sending and receiving ambassadors—entering into treaties and alliances, provided that no treaty of commerce shall be made whereby the legislative power of the respective States shall be restrained from imposing such imposts and duties on foreigners, as their own people are subjected to, or from prohibiting the exportation or importation of any species of goods or commodities whatsoever—of establishing rules for deciding all cases, what captures on land or water shall be legal, and in what manner prizes taken by land or naval forces in the service of the United States shall be divided or appropriated—of granting letters of marque and reprisal in times of peace— appointing courts for the trial of piracies and felonies committed on the high seas and establishing courts for receiving and determining finally appeals in all cases of captures, provided that no member of Congress shall be appointed a judge of any of the said courts.

The United States in Congress assembled shall also be the last resort on appeal in all disputes and differences now subsisting or that hereafter may arise between two or more States concerning boundary, jurisdiction or any other cause whatever; which authority shall always be exercised in the manner following. Whenever the legislative or executive authority or lawful agent of any State in controversy with another shall present a petition to Congress, stating the matter in question and praying for a hearing, notice thereof shall be given by order of Congress to the legislative or executive authority of the other State in controversy, and a day assigned for the appearance of the parties by their lawful agents, who shall then be directed to appoint by joint consent, commissioners or judges to constitute a court for hearing and determining the matter in question: but if they cannot agree, Congress shall name three persons out of each of the United States, and from the list of such persons each party shall alternately strike out one, the petitioners beginning, until the number shall be reduced to thirteen; and from that number not less than seven, nor more than nine names as Congress shall direct, shall in the presence of Congress be drawn out by lot, and the persons whose names shall be so drawn or any five of them, shall be commissioners or judges, to hear and finally determine the controversy, so always as a major part of the judges who shall hear the cause shall agree in the determination: and if either party shall neglect to attend at the day appointed, without showing reasons, which Congress shall judge sufficient, or being present shall refuse to strike, the Congress shall proceed to nominate three persons out of each State, and the Secretary of Congress shall strike in behalf of such party absent or refusing; and the judgment and sentence of the court to be appointed, in the manner before prescribed, shall be final and conclusive; and if any of the parties shall refuse to submit to the authority of such court, or to appear or defend their claim or cause, the court shall nevertheless proceed to pronounce sentence, or judgment, which shall in like manner be final or decisive, the judgment or sentence and other proceedings being in either case transmitted to Congress, and lodged among the acts of Congress for the security of the parties concerned: provided that every commissioner, before he sits in judgment, shall take an oath to be administered by one of the judges of the supreme or superior court of the State where the cause shall be tried, "well and truly to hear and determine the matter in question, according to the best of his judgment, without favour, affection or hope of reward:" provided also that no State shall be deprived of territory for the benefit of the United States.

All controversies concerning the private right of soil claimed under different grants of two or more States, whose jurisdiction as they may respect such lands, and the States which passed such grants are adjusted, the said grants or either of them being at the same time claimed to have originated antecedent to such settlement of jurisdiction, shall on the petition of either party to the Congress of the United States, be finally determined as near as may be in the same manner as is before prescribed for deciding disputes respecting territorial jurisdiction between different States.

The United States in Congress assembled shall also have the sole and exclusive right and power of regulating the alloy and value of coin struck by their own authority, or by that of the respective States—fixing the standard of weights and measures throughout the United States—regulating the trade and managing all affairs with the Indians, not members of any of the States, provided that the legislative right of any State within its own limits be not infringed or violated—establishing and regulating post-offices from one State to another, throughout all the United States, and exacting such postage on the papers passing thro' the same as may be requisite to defray the expenses of the said office—appointing all officers of the land forces, in the service of the United States, excepting regimental officers—appointing all the officers of the naval forces, and commissioning all officers whatever in the service of the United States—making rules for the government and regulation of the said land and naval forces, and directing their operations.

The United States in Congress assembled shall have authority to appoint a committee, to sit in the recess of Congress, to be denominated "a Committee of the States," and to consist of one delegate form each State; and to appoint such other committees and civil officers as may be necessary for managing the general affairs of the United States under their direction—to appoint one of their number to preside, provided that no person be allowed to serve in the office of president more than one year in any term of three years; to ascertain the necessary sums of money to be raised for the service of the United States, and to appropriate and apply the same for defraying the public expenses—to borrow money, or emit bills on the credit of the United States, transmitting every half year to the respective States an account of the sums of money so borrowed or emitted,—to build and equip a navy—to agree upon the number of land forces, and to make requisitions from each State for its quota, in proportion to the number of white inhabitants in such State; which requisition shall be binding, and thereupon the Legislature of each State shall appoint the regimental officers, raise the men and cloath, arm and equip them in a soldier like manner, at the expense of the United States; and the officers and men so cloathed, armed and equipped shall march to the place appointed, and within the time agreed on by the United States in Congress assembled: but if the United States in Congress assembled shall, on consideration of circumstances judge proper that any State should not raise men, or should raise a smaller number of men than the quota thereof, such extra number shall be raised, officered, cloathed, armed and equipped in the same manner as the quota of such State, unless the legislature of such State shall judge that such extra number cannot be safely spared out of the same, in which case they shall raise officer, cloath, arm and equip as many of such extra number as they judge can be safely spared. And the officers and men so cloathed, armed and equipped, shall march to the place appointed, and within the time agreed on by the United States in Congress assembled.

The United States in Congress assembled shall never engage in a war, nor grant letters of marque and reprisal in time of peace, nor enter into any treaties or alliances, nor coin money, nor regulate the value thereof, nor ascertain the sums and expenses necessary for the defence and welfare of the United States, or any of them, nor emit bills, nor borrow money on the credit of the United States, nor appropriate money, nor agree upon the number of vessels of war, to be built or purchased, or the number of land or sea forces to be raised, nor appoint a commander in chief of the army or navy, unless nine States assent to the same: nor shall a question on any other point, except for adjourning from day to day be determined, unless by the votes of a majority of the United States in Congress assembled.

The Congress of the United States shall have power to adjourn to any time within the year, and to any place within the United States, so that no period of adjournment be for a longer duration than the space of six months, and shall publish the journal of their proceedings monthly, except such parts thereof relating to treaties, alliances or military operations, as in their judgment require secresy; and the yeas and nays of the delegates of each State on any question shall be entered on the Journal, when it is desired by any delegate; and the delegates of a State, or any of them, at his or their request shall be furnished with a transcript of the said journal, except such parts as are above excepted, to lay before the Legislatures of the several States.

The legislative authority.

One delegate from each state—again, the smallest and poorest state may exert the same political "clout" as its biggest and richest brother state.

This "Committee of States" was the closest thing to an "executive authority." At one time about 100 committees existed, with authorities and functions overlapping and sometimes duplicating.

Congress could only make *requisitions* for troops.

One more indication of the status of blacks.

Paragraph 6. Note that important issues required consent of nine of the states. Five tiny states could thwart the wishes of three fourths of the population of the country. The obtaining of nine consenting votes was made even more difficult by the rule that state delegations which were evenly voted would be officially registered as not voting.

Article X

The committee of the States, or any nine of them, shall be authorized to execute, in the recess of Congress, such of the powers of Congress as the United States in Congress assembled, by the consent of nine States, shall from time to time think expedient to vest them with; provided that no power be delegated to the said committee, for the exercise of which, by the articles of confederation, the voice of nine States in the Congress of the United States assembled is requisite.

The extremely cautionary states' rights philosophy is again expressed here. The committee of states can only act with the approval of nine states.

Article XI

Canada acceding to this confederation, and joining in the measures of the United States, shall be admitted into, and entitled to all the advantages of this Union: but no other colony shall be admitted into the same, unless such admission be agreed to by nine States.

Article XII

All bills of credit emitted, monies borrowed and debts contracted by, or under the authority of Congress, before the assembling of the United States, in pursuance of the present confederation, shall be deemed and considered as a charge against the United States, for payment and satisfaction whereof the said United States, and the public faith are hereby solemnly pledged.

Compare with Paragraph 1 of Article VI of the Constitution.

Article XIII

Every State shall abide by the determinations of the United States in Congress assembled, on all questions which by this confederation are submitted to them. And the articles of this confederation shall be inviolably observed by every State, and the Union shall be perpetual; *nor shall any alteration at any time hereafter be made in any of them; unless such alteration be agreed to in a Congress of the United States, and be afterwards confirmed by the Legislatures of every State.*

And whereas it has pleased the Great Governor of the world to incline the hearts of the Legislatures we respectively represent in Congress, to approve of, and to authorize us to ratify the said articles of confederation and perpetual union. Know ye that we the undersigned delegates, by virtue of the power and authority to us given for that purpose, do by these presents, in the name and in behalf of our respective constituents, fully and entirely ratify and confirm each and every of the said articles of confederation and perpetual union, and all and singular the matters and things therein contained: and we do further solemnly plight and engage the faith of our respective constituents, that they shall abide by the determinations of the United States in Congress assembled, on all questions, which by the said confederation are submitted to them. And that the articles thereof shall be inviolably observed by the States we respectively represent, and that the Union shall be perpetual.

In witness whereof we have hereunto set our hands in Congress. Done at Philadelphia in the State of Pennsylvania the ninth day of July in the year of our Lord one thousand seven hundred and seventy-eight, and in the third year of the independence of America.

The italicized phrase probably doomed the Articles of Confederation and brought on the present Constitution. Because of the diverse interests, it was virtually impossible to obtain the unanimous consent necessary to amend the Articles. All other faults of the Articles could have been corrected through Amendment.

Answers to Questions

Chapter 1

1. No. Foreigners, slaves, and women were excluded.
2. The Romans of the period of the *Pax Romana*.
3. It was an agreement between the king and people to live up to terms of their feudal contract.
4. With destruction of the Holy Roman Empire, states within the empire were able to develop common patriotic ties and become individual nations.
5. As the first *national* written constitution of the modern type. It was also a reasonable prototype of the U.S. Constitution.
6. They bound themselves to stay together and form a civil body politic—the Mayflower Compact.
7. The modern nation-state was made possible with collapse of the Holy Roman Empire.
8. It was not written. It evolved over many centuries from custom, tradition, Parliamentary Acts, common law, judicial decisions, etc.
9. The organizational structure of the Calvinist Church is based upon consent of the governed.
10. The Fundamental Orders of Connecticut of 1639, binding three cities into a common government.
11. All were illegal.

12. It could be considered the first written constitution of the modern type.
13. After a decade of Commonwealth rule, the Stuart king, Parliament, and the Anglican church were returned to power.
14. The king's powers would henceforth be limited; Parliament was in the ascendancy.
15. It stressed the general agreement that the Articles were unable to handle the problem of commercial regulation. The convention was a sort of batting practice for the Constitutional Convention.
16. Any amendment required unanimous approval of all thirteen colonies.
17. A unicameral, or one-chamber, legislature.
18. They were western Massachusetts farmers, many of whom had fought in the War of Independence and returned to a hard-money squeeze that found them underrepresented in the state legislature.
19. Because it was the will of the people, who mistrusted any king or governor.
20. Though the cause was just, a spread of that type of violence could have led to anarchy.
21. Cabal and cabinet.
22. How to revolt against unjust rulers.

Chapter 2

1. Forty-three.
2. Benjamin Franklin, at eighty-one.
3. Because she set a brilliant example of sending qualified men.
4. Governor Edmund Randolph.
5. Fellow delegates, Yates and Lansing, consistently outvoted him, two to one.
6. George Washington.
7. Charles Beard.
8. That the Constitution reflects the influence of wealthy and propertied delegates.
9. Thomas Jefferson, John Adams, Tom Paine, John Hancock, Patrick Henry, John Jay, Samuel Adams.
10. No. A secrecy rule was enforced. There were no blacks, Indians, women, Jews, or labor representatives, and only two Catholics.
11. A parliamentary device allowing delegates to speak off the record.
12. William Paterson of New Jersey.
13. The Connecticut Compromise, whose principal feature gave small states two votes in the Senate.

14. The British system, with an upper chamber elected for life and a king-like executive.
15. Gouverneur Morris of Pennsylvania.
16. He declined to serve as a delegate and led Virginia Anti-Federalists in the campaign against ratification.
17. James Madison.
18. There was no money for expenses. Finally, a wealthy member of the delegation agreed to pay the bill.
19. They were regarded as property, and counted as a fraction of a person in determining representation.
20. The decision to devote complete attention to the Virginia Plan ahead of any other business.

Chapter 3

1. Federalists.
2. Members of Congress would be asked to vote themselves out of office.
3. Nine.
4. No. Example: Of Pennsylvania's 430,000 citizens, 70,000 were eligible, 13,000 voted.
5. *State*, not federal, rules applied. Eligible voters voted for delegates to state conventions. These delegates usually voted as instructed, but occasionally made up their own minds.
6. Burdened with heavy mortgages, they wished to pay off in inflated dollars. A strong central government would likely curb inflation.
7. Bad weather and bad roads kept Anti-Federalist rural voters at home. Generally, townspeople had an easier time getting to the polls.
8. New Hampshire.
9. Delaware, New Jersey, and Georgia.
10. Publius.
11. Governor Edmund Randolph.
12. New York.
13. Favor.
14. Rhode Island.
15. None. He was in Paris.
16. She needed military help from a strong government against the Indians.
17. Madison, Hamilton, and Jay.
18. New York was faring well under the Articles. Because of her fine harbor and strategically placed waterways, she was able to exact heavy tolls on shipping. This advantage would be wiped out under a single union.

19. Alexander Hamilton.

20. Leader of the opposition in Virginia.

21. Sovereignty.

22. They favored it. They were pleased with the compromise that gave them equal representation in the Senate; and they were not individually powerful enough to survive by themselves.

23. They were underrepresented, because delegates were selected according to the formula for choosing members of the Confederation Congress, where urban areas usually were overrepresented.

24. Concerned about certain basic rights and freedoms, Massachusetts was persuaded to ratify only after she attached a suggested "Bill of Rights" and was given assurance that it would be addressed. Other doubtful states followed suit.

25. There would have been a United States *without* George Washington or Thomas Jefferson.

Chapter 4

1. They could be changed only by unanimous vote of all thirteen colonies, making them virtually unamendable.

2. Proposal and ratification.

3. Proposal. Congress proposed only 33 of the first 10,104 it considered. Of the 33 proposed, 26 were ratified.

4. 1. By a two-thirds vote of both houses of Congress.
2. By a national convention assembled by Congress upon application of two-thirds of the states.

5. No. But the balanced-budget amendment has a chance.

6. None.

7. By approval of three-fourths of the state legislatures.

8. Approval of specially called conventions in three-fourths of the states.

9. Yes, with the Twenty-first Amendment.

10. A bill is passed by simple majority vote and sent to the president. An amendment must pass Congress by a two-thirds majority, then sent on for approval by three-fourths of the states.

11. Yes. By wielding their power as party leaders and using the prestige of their offices.

12. Yes. It may propose an amendment to change the Constitution.

13. The eleventh, the fourteenth, the sixteenth, and the twenty-sixth.

14. The initial seven-year ratification period was extended for thirty-nine months, setting what some called a "dangerous precedent."

15. Generally, it has refused to act, deferring to Congress.
16. The twenty-sixth, giving eighteen-year-olds the right to vote. It was proposed in March 1971 and was ratified by July 1.
17. Thomas Jefferson
18. *Chisholm v. Georgia.*
19. Twelve. Two were not ratified.
20. Only seven out of thirty-three.

Answers to Amendment Questions

The Bill of Rights

1.	2	5.	7	9.	3
2.	4	6.	5	10.	8
3.	6	7.	10	11.	5
4.	9	8.	1	12.	1

The Other Amendments

1.	19	8.	12	15.	14
2.	23	9.	18	16.	22
3.	11	10.	21	17.	16
4.	26	11.	24	18.	Speaker of the House
5.	17	12.	13	19.	their state legislatures
6.	25	13.	20	20.	13th
7.	13	14.	15		

Chapter 5

1. Only one—the Supreme Court. All other courts are to be established by Congress.
2. The Ellsworth Judiciary Act of 1789.
3. Franklin Roosevelt.
4. There are eighty-six district courts and eleven appellate divisions.
5. Congress.
6. Thomas Jefferson.
7. The lack of a federal judiciary had been one of the major flaws of the Articles of Confederation.
8. Through the power of appointment.
9. The Senate may refuse to confirm an appointment, or a judicial appointee may decide cases in a different manner than the president had anticipated.

10. Thurgood Marshall.
11. The power of the courts to declare laws unconstitutional.
12. John Marshall.
13. Owen Roberts and Charles Evans Hughes.
14. The Court found various aspects of the legislation to be unconstitutional, seriously impairing some New Deal programs.
15. Roosevelt proposed a court-packing plan that met with widespread opposition.
16. George Washington, with ten.
17. Thirty-four years.
18. Earl Warren.
19. Reverse discrimination.
20. *Brown v. Board of Education of Topeka*, *Baker v. Carr*, and *Miranda v. Arizona*.

Chapter 6

1. *McCulloch v. Maryland*.
2. *Gibbons v. Ogden*.
3. The case is listed in volume #278 of *United States Reports*, beginning on page 372; the particular citation is on page 374; the decision was rendered in 1987.
4. Implied powers.
5. *Gibbons v. Ogden*.
6. Separate but equal.
7. State laws, primarily in the South, that enforced separate facilities (bathroom, drinking fountains, buses, etc.) for blacks and whites.
8. John Marshall Harlan.
9. Because of Marshall's record favoring slavery.
10. A single, pregnant woman who wanted an abortion and whose suit against the state of Texas wound up in the Supreme Court.
11. *Marbury v. Madison*.
12. Clear and present danger.
13. Daniel Webster.
14. *Weeks v. U.S.*
15. Evidence illegally obtained may not be used in federal court.
16. *Baker v. Carr*.
17. Emergence of the black voter.
18. Hands off.

19. Three of his own appointees voted against him.
20. The president resigned.
21. He had been an assistant to Attorney General John Mitchell, one of the Watergate defendants.
22. *Brown v. Board of Education of Topeka.*
23. NAACP—National Association for the Advancement of Colored People.
24. There was bitter opposition by some factions for many years.
25. Earl Warren.
26. Because he was a slave and not a citizen; only citizens could sue in federal court.
27. The Missouri Compromise.
28. Because, as a slave, he was merely *property.*
29. In *McCulloch v. Maryland,* 1819, Marshall interpreted the clause in developing the doctrine of implied powers. He ruled that a need for a federal bank existed and was fully justified, though *not* listed as an enumerated power.
30. The "due process" and "equal protection of the laws" clauses of the Fourteenth Amendment.

Chapter 7

1. The Founding Fathers considered the House the most important element of the government, ahead of the Senate, Executive and Judiciary. The House is "closer to home" and its members are more responsive to the people because house elections are every two years.
2. The House impeaches, and the Senate conducts the trial.
3. The chief justice of the United States.
4. By a two-thirds vote of both houses of Congress.
5. No. Article II, Section 2, specifically forbids it.
6. Thirty-five years.
7. To *make* treaties? Yes. But Article II, Section 2 requires that a treaty, to become the law of the land, must be approved by a two-thirds vote of the Senate. In addition, the House may *unofficially* "veto" a treaty by refusing to appropriate funds to carry it out.
8. No. An exception was made in Article II, Section 1 for anyone who was a citizen "at the time of the adoption of this Constitution."
9. Because the wage setter(s) would in effect be able to reward or punish the president.
10. No.

11. Because Article 2, Section 1 forbids a presidential increase "during the period for which he shall have been elected. . . ."

12. Though the veto is a power of the *Executive*, the Founding Fathers believed it was more closely allied with the *Legislative* Branch.

Answers to Constitution Questions

1.	two	14.	b
2.	7, 25	15.	b
3.	30, 7	16.	c
4.	vice president	17.	c
5.	tie	18.	b
6.	House, Senate	19.	f
7.	chief justice	20.	c
8.	state governor	21.	a
9.	state governor, writ of election	22.	b
		23.	c
10.	House	24.	c
11.	President, two-thirds, Senate	25.	e
12.	President	26.	b
13.	c	27.	a

Glossary/Index

Affirmative action Policies that extend favorable treatment to members of minorities to make up for past discriminations. (Examples: Alloting a disproportionate number of new jobs; admitting students with lower grade point averages.) 90

Annapolis Convention A 1787 gathering that highlighted weaknesses of the Articles of Confederation.

Anti-Federalists Those who opposed ratificaton of the Constitution. 26, 28, 31, 34, 35, 42–43, 95

Appellant The party who appeals an unfavorable court decision to a court of review (appellate).

Appellee The original winner of the above case who stands to lose his decision if the verdict is overturned. Also known as the *respondent*.

Armed forces 9, 10, 32

Articles of Confederation The written Constitution of the United States, 1780–1788. 7, 9–11, 157–67

Attainder, bill of A legislative act pronouncing a person guilty (usually of treason) without benefit of trial and prescribing outlawry or death and attaintment (dishonor and loss of all civil rights). Applied in England in the Middle Ages and early modern times. Guarded against in Art. I (Sec. 9 and 10). 129, 130, 136

Bicameral A parliamentary body consisting of two parts or houses. In the U.S., the federal Congress and all state legislatures except unicameral Nebraska.

Bill A proposed law presented to a legislative body. When duly passed, it becomes a *law*.

Blacks 25, 50–54, 83, 86–87, 100, 102–3; *see also* Slavery.

Canada 147

Capitation tax Literally, a tax on one's head. A tax fixed equally on each person. Art. I, Sec. 9 prohibited this type of tax, but this prohibition was erased by the 16th Amendment, permitting the income tax. 43, 63, 129

177

Cases, Supreme Court

Civil suit As opposed to a criminal
suit, an action by one party to protect a
possession, secure a legal right, or repair or redress a wrong. Damages may
be assessed, but no fine or imprisonment is imposed. (Example: Suit to re-
strain nearby factory from blackening
one's house by heavy smoke emissions.)

Clauses
   Commerce Clause (Art. 1, Sec. 8,
P-3) "The Congress shall have power.
. . . To regulate Commerce with foreign
Nations, and among the several States,
and with the Indian Tribes;" A source
of enormous power. 84, 89, 127

   Due Process Clause (14th amendment) "No state shall . . . abridge the
privileges or immunities of citizens of
the United States; nor . . . deprive any
person of life, liberty, or property,
without due process of law;" 54, 60,
62, 88

   Establishment clause (1st amendment) "Congress shall make no law respecting an establishment of religion,
or prohibiting the free exercise
thereof;" 51

   Equal protection of the laws clause
(14th amendment) "Nor shall (any
state) deny to any person . . . the equal
protection of the laws." (Sec. 1) 60, 62

   Necessary and proper clause (Art.
1, Sec. 8) Authorizes Congress "to
make all Laws which be necessary and
proper for carrying into Execution the
foregoing Powers, and all other Powers
vested by this Constitution. . . ." A
source of great power. 10, 98, 128

   Supremacy clause (Art. VI, P-2)
"This Constitution and the Laws of the
United States . . . and all Treaties made
. . . shall be the supreme law of the
land;" The basis of many cases where
state and federal laws conflict. 83, 84,
98–99, 140

Construction
   Loose—The liberal or "easy" interpretation that insists that certain powers
can properly be "implied" from other
specified powers. John Marshall was a
loose constructionist. 84
   Strict—The interpretation that argues that only powers specifically delegated to the national government are

allowable. States' righters, such as George Wallace, are strict constructionists who cite the 10th Amendment. 99

Corruption of blood Mentioned in Art. III, Sec. 3. In English history, a bill of attainder also "attainted" members of the victim's family. 136

Double jeopardy A person tried once and found not guilty of a crime would be placed in double jeopardy if he were again tried for the same crime in the same court. Forbidden by the 5th and 14th Amendments. Where the crime is an offense against a federal and a state law, he could be tried in both federal and state courts. 54

Due process The standard steps provided by law for a judicial proceeding that take into account the basic constitutional rights guaranteed every citizen brought before the bar of justice. 54, 62, 88

Equal Rights Amendment 42, 44, 46–49

Eminent domain The right of a government to take private property. Also, the procedure by which this action is accomplished and proper payment established. 53

Enumerated powers Those powers specifically authorized by the Constitution. For instance, the powers of the Congress are enumerated (Art. I, Sec. 8), 127; presidential powers are named (Art. II, Sec 2), 133–34; judicial power is delegated (Art. III, Sec 2). 136

Exclusionary rule Prohibits admission as evidence all information obtained in violation of due process guidelines. 109–10

Ex post facto law On Wednesday George J. Citizen is convicted for having fished on Monday in a section of the river that on Tuesday was declared off-limits for fishing by the city council. A law enacted and applied after an act has been committed. 129, 130

Federalist Papers Classic essays favoring ratification of the U.S. Constitution. 29, 30, 96–97

Federalists Those who favored ratification of the U.S. Constitution (not to be confused with members of the Federalist party, who were also called Federalists). 26, 28–29, 32–33, 34

Felony A serious crime. Conviction may result in imprisonment, usually for a year or more, and a fine, or both.

Founding Fathers Members of the Philadelphia Constitutional Convention of 1787; especially the 39 signers. 48, 84, 117, 155–56; Also see Chapter 2.

Fundamental Orders of Connecticut The written document under which the colonists of several towns in Connecticut consented to be governed in 1639. Probably the first modern written constitution. 4

Great Compromise (Connecticut Compromise) 21–22, 31

Gerrymander Formed from the words "Gerry" and "salamander," this term refers to a legislative district geographically distorted for political purposes (election districts are supposed to be approximately even in size and shape). Gov. Elbridge Gerry of Massachusetts had a hand in the shaping of a salamander-shape district in 1812. 22

Habeas corpus, writ of (Latin for "you have the body") A writ directing an official to produce a prisoner in court and explain why the prisoner is being held. 129

High seas Waters where ships of all nations are allowed to sail. 127, 154

Humble Petition and Advice The written English constitution of the late 1650s that was a total failure, thus being a factor in bringing about the demand for the Restoration (of the Stuart monarchy) in 1660. 4

Impeachment 96, 121–22, 134–35

Implied powers The "necessary and proper" clause (Art. I, Sec. 8) *implies* that if Congress is responsible for certain *enumerated* powers, it must be allowed to implement its task by passing non-enumerated legislation. 84, 128

Indentured servants Usually adult whites bound by contract to labor for a specified period of time. There were three types: (a) convicts; (b) those lured or kidnapped from a foreign country; and (c) those who freely agreed to the arrangement in order to pay for their passage to America. 26, 119

Indictment A written accusation, handed over to a court by a grand jury, charging an individual with a crime. The indictment (true bill) is made following hearings and merely states that the grand jury believes the evidence shown by the prosecutor is sufficient to warrant bringing the accused to trial. The student must bear in mind that the indictment makes no judgment on innocence or guilt. 53

Injunction A court order requiring an individual or a party to do something (or refrain from doing something). Violation may result in a citation for contempt of court.

In re In regard to, concerning. Method of entitling a case in which a single party makes an application on his own behalf. (Also called *"ex parte"*— by one party.)

Instrument of Government The written English Constitution of 1653 under which the Lord Protector, Oliver Cromwell, was the executive authority who received advice from a Council of State. Legislative authority was vested in a Parliament. The experiment was a short-lived failure. Among nations, it was the first written constitution of the modern type. 4

Jail A holding place for prisoners awaiting trial or transfer to prison, or for persons convicted of misdemeanors.

Jurisdiction
Appellate—Authority of a court to hear appeals from a lower court. 96, 135, 136
Original—Authority to hear cases originally. 96, 135

Lame duck An official whose influence is lessened because he will soon leave office, usually because he has just lost an election. 67; Also see the 20th Amendment.

Letters of marque and reprisal (Art. I, Sec. 10) An official government document giving a citizen the right to seize goods (and sometimes citizens) of another nation; a document allowing an individual to charter a ship with which to wage war (and keep the proceeds) against enemy vessels. A prohibition on the *states*. 130

Libel A defamatory *written* statement.

Mandamus, writ of (Latin for "we command") A court order commanding an administrative or judicial official to perform an action associated with his office. 95, 96

Maverick In politics, an independent who cannot be branded by a party label. From Samuel Maverick, a Texas rancher who neglected to brand his calves.

"Midnight" appointments Appointments of John Adams which led to *Marbury* decision. 95

Misdemeanor An offense less serious than a felony, usually punished with a fine or short jail sentence.

Missouri Compromise The Act of Congress of 1820 whereby (a) provision was made for Missouri to enter the union as a slave state; (b) Maine was admitted as a free state; and (c) slavery was excluded from all Louisiana Purchase territory north of 30° 60' except in Missouri. The Compromise thus allowed for admission of two states, kept the number of slave and free states

from this tax belonged to the king. To promote free trade among the states, Art. I, Sec. 10, prohibits *any state* from levying tonnage. 130

True bill The written report of the grand jury that specifies an indictment. 53

Veto (Art. I, Sec. 7) 80, 125

Virginia Plan (Randolph Plan) 19–20

Writ of certiori A formal written request to a court of appeals for a review of a lower court decision.

About the Author

Joseph Keenan was educated at Chicago's DePaul University, where he was Director of Bookstores for 30 years. For 18 of those years he was also a member of the History Department.

The author took early retirement in 1982, and moved to Sun City, Arizona. Though he loved the lifestyle, he missed the classroom. After one year of "retirement" he began teaching again at local branches of Rio Salado and Arizona State University. His new experiences took him to Perryville State Prison and Luke Air Force Base. He also converted many articles into lecture form, and appeared before service clubs and on radio talk shows. The lecture titles ranged from "How to Live with a Punster," to "The Magic of Words," to "How's This for Openers" (a collection of opening lines of news stories, particularly of sports page gems), to "Murder in the Forest," an unbelievable concentration camp atrocity which unfolds like a detective story.

Keenan's easy-to-read *The Constitution of the United States* has had a steady market since its publication in 1975. After several minor updates, he has expanded and thoroughly revised this bicentennial edition.

A NOTE ON THE TYPE

The text of this book was set in 10/12 Times Roman, a film version of the face designed by Stanley Morison, which was first used by *The Times* (of London) in 1932. Part of Morison's special intent for Times Roman was to create a face that was editorially neutral. It is an especially compact, attractive, and legible typeface, which has come to be seen as the "most important type design of the twentieth century."

Composed by Weimer Typesetting Co., Inc.

Printed and bound by Arcata Graphics/Kingsport